REA

Harry Elmer Barnes
As I Knew Him

Harry Elmer Barnes
As I Knew Him

Robert H. Barnes

High Plains Publishing Company

HIGH PLAINS PUBLISHING COMPANY, INC.
Post Office Box 1860
Worland, Wyoming 82401

Contents

Contents

Acknowledgments

Without good friends, the old ones and the new ones I found as a result of this effort, this book would not have progressed beyond a few random short stories, full of misspelled words, mixed metaphors and the like. Dr. Gene M. Gressley, for many years the director of the American Heritage Center at the University of Wyoming and a long-time friend of a fellow historian, Harry Elmer Barnes, continually encouraged me. Dad's letters and related memorabilia, preserved in the Center at Laramie, were readily available to me through Gene, and our continuing exchange of classic Barnes tales did much to keep the creative juices flowing.

My sister, Barbara Tilford, not only reminded me of many long-forgotten family stories, but breathed fresh energy into my labors when it was most needed. The same can be said of Roy F. Ames, who grew up with us on the farm and remains an important part of our lives.

Acknowledgments

Clee Richeson helped give life and action to my thoughts and words. Anne Kesselman's initial proofreading helped resurrect the manuscript from an abyss filled with my third-grade spelling. The frontispiece is the work of a longtime friend, Virginia True, for decades professor of art at Cornell University. She was particularly close to HEB during his mid-years and well loved by all of us.

Finally, accolades to my family for patiently listening to some of the stories a multitude of times. And a special accolade to my wife, Beverly, for her love and fortitude in not only listening, but also for saving my life during a serious bout with cancer while the book was in progress—in the words of one of HEB's fundamentalist hymns, her "love lifted me."

R.H.B.

Introduction

"Help, help, there's a mouse in my bed." The words erupted from my mouth in the middle of the night. As a four-year-old I was afraid of the dark, would crawl down the hall to Grandmother's room, and clamber up on her bed to lie securely at her feet. She never objected, but Dad felt it was an unbecoming sign of weakness for a child at the advanced age of four. Thus, I had been warned to cease such childish behavior, and for several nights I had succeeded. But that night I had been awakened by something furry crawling down my shoulder, along my side, and down my leg to my feet. My cry was emphatic and must have carried a compelling note. Within a few seconds Dad appeared, clad only in a tank top, his favorite sleeping attire. Gently he addressed his terrified child: "There's no goddamn mouse in your bed!" And in order to show me, he pulled the blanket and sheet down to my feet with all the nurturing grace that Lee Iaccoca might display on unveiling a new Chrysler. To his surprise and my relief, a small gray object leaped from the bed and disappeared out the door and down the hall. Dad's only comment was a loud "Jesus Christ!" followed by the admonishment, "Go back to sleep." Although generally a fair and considerate man, he was loath to burden himself with the guilt associated with admissions of error.

This episode seems an appropriate introduction to the Barnes family, particularly my Dad, myself, and our relationship. It is one of the earliest in my memory and a starting place for recalling a series of happenings from my childhood through my youth, events that occurred more than a half century ago. This is not an in-depth psychoanalytic account of my growing up or an analysis of a father-son relationship. Many traumatic episodes are omitted. It is meant to be amusing as well as authentic: the details give a flavor of American culture from the mid-1920s through the mid-1960s as viewed by a boy raised during those eventful years. It is also intended to picture one segment in the life of a remarkable renaissance man, who retained all the earthiness of nineteenth–century rural America from which he and several generations of his family had sprung. In part, it is inspired by Clarence Day's *Life with Father*,[1] a book I read with great enjoyment in my teens. Further inducement came by way of Fredrick Lewis Allen's *Only Yesterday*[2] and *Since Yesterday*[3]. The latter's animated accounts of the 1920s and 1930s influenced and expanded my memories of those years.

Harry Elmer Barnes, my father, was born in the summer of 1889 to Lulu Short Barnes and William Henry Barnes, Jr., on the family farm in upstate New York; he was the first of three sons. The Old Family Homestead, as it was known by my time, was located on a 100-acre tract, 10 miles north of Auburn. That city had basked for many years in the glory of having been the home of Abraham Lincoln's secretary of state, William Seward, of Alaskan fame. Three miles farther to the north lay Port Byron (named after Lord

The Old Family Homestead (circa 1890)

Byron), a port on the Erie Canal, the waterway that settled the West. In 1889, the traffic on the canal was still moved by mules urged along a towpath by the cracking whips of "mule skinners." Port Byron was a prosperous hamlet that had bred such notables as Isaac Singer, inventor of the sewing machine, and Henry Wells of Wells Fargo fame. It was the site of the high school where all the farm youth possessed of lofty ambition spent four years of dedicated effort, following eight years in one-room rural schools. In the elementary grades they had been taught by determined schoolmarms and raw-boned farm boys just out of high school. Many of the latter hoped to earn enough money in the non-farming season to allow a try at Syracuse University or that Ivy League institution perched high and far above the deep blue waters of Cayuga Lake and known to the local Christians as a "hot bed of atheism"—Cornell.

The Barnes homestead was an adequate home for two families, with separate facilities for each. Dad's paternal grandfather and grandmother lived in the front of the house, and his father and mother and their brood of three boys lived in the back section. Dad, an adorable and precocious first grandchild, was taken over by his grandmother, indulged and coddled, and according to his mother's accounts, "badly spoiled." The older couple were relaxed, easy-going and semi-retired, enjoyed cards, an occasional drink, and were not overly infused with Christian

H.E.B.—The favorite grandchild

zeal. The younger couple, Dad's parents, were struggling, pious to a fault, and deadset against the cardinal sins of smoking, drinking,dancing, and cards. Church attendance was mandatory on Sunday morning and Wednesday evening, and the scriptures were taken quite literally and in accordance with the fundamentalist teachings of the Campellite elders of the

Father and Mother Barnes

Church of the Disciples of Christ. Although greatly influenced by his grandfather and grandmother, Harry fell readily into the strict piety of his mother and worried much about his beloved grandfather's everlasting soul, given as he was to drinking, smoking, and general lack of Christian enthusiasm. He was even suspected of atheistic leanings.

To support two families on less than 100 acres is testimony to diligence and a fertile soil. It also suggests a less than opulent life-style. And indeed that was the case, with Dad's father working off-season as a prison guard at the famous Auburn State Prison and as a teacher in the nearby, one-room rural school. All three boys worked on the farm, and Harry worked for two years after high school as a construction engineer and rural schoolteacher to save for college; he was driven with the ambition of becoming a high school history teacher. When he left for Syracuse University in September 1909, it was with the meager savings from those efforts, a used overcoat and suit, along with a family gift of $25 and their blessings. At Syracuse, he clerked in the drugstore of a family friend and lived with the friend's family. Summers he worked 12- and 15-hour shifts as a cannery foreman in Auburn, daily riding his bicycle 10 miles each way from the homestead.

Syracuse University was a well-regarded, solid, Methodist school, and Dad appears to have taken advantage of almost everything available in history, sociology, and economics. It opened a vast new intellectual world for him. However in the process, to quote his pious mother, "Harry lost Christ." Yet, despite this, she was tremendously proud of him. A bright, although relatively uneducated woman, she undoubtedly appreciated more than anyone his graduating summa cum laude. I think she also quietly applauded his continuing on to a master's degree at Syracuse and a Ph.D. at Columbia. He was blessed in being there at a time when the intellectual center for many of the social sciences resided with the brilliant faculty gathered on Morningside Heights.

Dad was the archetype of the young intellectual of the World War I era, grounded in the rigorous and austere rural frontier culture of post–Civil War America and suddenly thrust into the heady ferment of the twentieth century. He found himself rubbing shoulders with, and often leading, the East Coast intelligentsia of the period stretching from the days of Wilson, Harding, and the flappers through Prohibition, the Great Depression, World War II, and into the early years of the Cold War. In this forty-year period, he taught at Harvard, Columbia, Clark, Smith, Amherst, Cornell, and Colorado; was numbered among the original faculty of the New School for Social Research; and was a founding member of the American Civil Liberties Union. He was a leader in the field of World War I and II revisionist history and one of the chief editorial writers for the Scripps-Howard newspaper chain and the *New York World Telegram*. As a public lecturer, he was in constant demand nationally. As a writer, he produced some forty volumes ranging in subject from *The Genesis of the World War*[4] to *The Twilight of Christianity*[5]. He left a rich legacy of correspondence and reminiscences with such friends and acquaintances as H. L. Mencken, George Jean Nathan, Charles Austin Beard, Sinclair Lewis, Clarence Darrow, H. G. Wells, John Dewey, Will Rogers, and many others.

Dad's personal and family life was a heady brew

of frenetic activity and an admixture of behaviors drawn from the mores and folkways of rural nineteenth century America and of the East Coast of the 1920s through the 1960s. His first wife, my mother, to whom he was married for more than twenty years, was a high school classmate and the sister of his closest boyhood friend. His second wife was much more representative of the East Coast society of the 1930s. Their marriage lasted for more than thirty years— until his death in 1968. With the second marriage came the invaluable addition of a girl to the family, a step-sister who shared with me many of the episodes recounted in this book. Other events and important parts of my adolescence and early adult life were also shared and enhanced by a bright and energetic young man, four years my senior, who was in many ways an older brother. He lived with us on the upstate farm and has remained a close and valued friend through many years since the early 1930s. Both saved me from the limitations attached to the status of only child. They have also sharpened my memory in recounting many of the occurrences in this book.

Where we lived also came to reflect the two sides of Dad's cultural background. I was born in 1921 and raised in Northampton, a delightful, small New England college town, the site of Smith College. We moved in the early 1930s to Tarrytown, a suburb of New York City, and then to upstate New York to a farm one-quarter mile from the Old Family Homestead. During the 1940s and 1950s the Barnes family lived outside Cooperstown, New York, on a farm overlooking the broad expanse of Otsego Lake, famed as the Glimmer Glass of James Fenimore Cooper's Leatherstocking Tales. From the late 1950s Dad occupied his final home, located on the California coast; it was a small ranch above the Pacific, a few miles west of Malibu. In his choice of where to live, Dad expressed his ties to the culture of his youth: post–Civil War rural America. To me the unique beauty of the environment in which we lived did indeed constitute growing up in paradise. Like many youthful experiences, the appreciation is often greater in retrospect.

Being raised by this energetic, highly educated, articulate, opinionated father, with his one leg planted firmly in the agrarian past and the other floating erratically in the rapidly changing intellectual climate of mid-twentieth-century America, was often unsettling, sometimes frightening, occasionally maddening but never boring. This book is dedicated to those memories. The episodes, as they unfold, have the vividness of events that often seem to have happened "only yesterday."

Chapter 1
The Ball

"Play ball!" and the nine super athletes of Port Byron High School, wildly cheered on by twelve cherub-faced, bloomer-bottomed classmates, took the field against Weedsport High, the always odds-on favorite from 8 miles east along the towpath of the Erie Canal. The battery that day, and for the previous three seasons, was Barnes (pitcher) and Stone (catcher). They were backed up by eight other ball players, all this school of thirty could muster, in toto, to celebrate the great American pastime. But in 1904 the "upstate" locals probably derived more excitement from cheering their high school heroes than TV's couch potatoes experienced watching the Oakland Athletics overwhelm the San Francisco Giants four straight, with the addition of an earthquake and several six-packs of Miller's Lite!

Port Byron High School cheerleaders

The battery was an all-family affair, with the catcher, my beloved uncle-to-be, Fred Stone, and the pitcher, my father of seventeen years later. That day, however, their imaginations were on matters other than future family entanglements. Weedsport was "blowing out" the boys from Lord Byron's port on the Old Canal, and soon the word of this disgrace would travel down the towpath by mule skinner to the hated metropolis 8 miles east.

As the battery of Barnes and Stone was experiencing its greatest debacle, a somewhat more newsworthy event was being acted out in New York, that other great port of the Empire State. The cheers of Yankee fans were building to a crescendo as the great Jack Chesbro retired the last Athletic and won his forty-first game of the season—a record never to be topped, although that fact was obviously not known to the stadium fans, lacking as they did an announcer with a *Guiness Book of Records* and a time machine to scan the future.[*] But it was a coincidence, the strangeness of which is probably of note only to me—one who often dwells on such happenstance.

Years and wars and presidents pass—Roosevelt, Taft, Wilson, Harding—and we find ourselves comfortably ensconced in the era of Coolidge and in the very hometown of "Silent Cal": Northampton. I am seven and already indoctrinated with the gospel that "my Dad" is one of the great ball players of the ages. Today he is starring on the playing fields of Smith College, performing on his, or at least my, "field of dreams." Early in his tenure at Smith he had organized an annual game between the girls and the faculty. In order to add color to the occasion he had arranged, in some way unknown to me but typical of him, for the legendary Jack Chesbro, who had long since retired to the nearby Berkshires, to pitch for the students. And guess who this all-time great was pitching against—none other than my Dad. That was the strangeness of the coincidence of that day in 1904: the world's two premier pitchers—Jack Chesbro and

---

[*]Jack Chesbro played with the Pittsburgh Pirates from 1899 to 1902 and with the New York Yankees from 1903 to 1909. In 1904 he won a total of 41 games for the season, a record never equaled. He is also given dubious credit for inventing the "spitball."

my Dad—one had his ultimate triumph and the other his greatest defeat!

I remember very little of the Smith College game of 1928—only that Dad hit a home run and that we had the "Jack Chesbro Ball" in the family from that day forward. It was a common, everyday ball, one that an outfielder on the Smith team had retrieved and given ceremoniously to Dad to commemorate his monumental drive. After the game Jack considerately signed the ball as he probably had thousands of others.

The years rolled by, and my interest in the game and Dad's interest in the "Ball" waned. The Barnes family moved more than once and at the end of the 1930s settled in Cooperstown, New York. By chance the "Ball," along with some well-worn catchers' and fielders' mitts, survived all the moves and backyard scrimmages. As a result of being stuffed in dusty garage corners, the "Ball" was blemished, and Jack Chesbro's signature was mostly worn away because we had thoughtlessly placed the ball in service during pick-up games when it was the only available sphere in the box.

"Where the hell is that goddamned ball?" greeted me one crisp, early spring morning fifty years ago. For a moment I was lost and then the vision of the "Ball" and all its symbolism flooded my memory, reinforced by my second cup of Dad's double-strength instant coffee. I swallowed my last gulp and headed for the garage at the summer house where I had last been the "Ball" two years earlier. On the way, I began to grasp his renewed interest in the "Ball," as attested to by the vehemence of Dad's query. The local gentry, led by the heirs of the Singer Sewing Machine Company, the State Historical Society, and with the sanction of both major leagues, had established the Baseball Hall of Fame. What would be more appropriate than to have a donation from the town's most famous resident author, not to mention Port Byron High School's fabled (sic) pitcher, albeit of another era.

The "Ball" was located, but its emergence brought forth another loud bellow: "Where in the hell is Jack's signature?" I reminded Dad of all the times he and I had played catch and knocked out ground balls over Jack's autograph for the past twenty years, but he seemed not to hear. To help him, I unfortunately added, "If you are going to donate it, you can just say that Jack was the inventor of the 'spitball' and removed his signature with his own sputum before giving it to us. That makes it more authentic." This lame attempt at humor was totally unappreciated, and with a few more blasphemous bursts, Dad set off at a trot to one of his studies. A few minutes later he emerged a changed man with a broad and satisfied smile on his face. "There, Bo [his term of affection when he felt kindly toward me], that is a hell of a lot better signature than the old cuss ever signed himself." He proudly showed me a fresh rendition of the Jack Chesbro signature on that scuffed but venerable ball.

And so, a relic from my father's "field of dreams" may still reside in the Baseball Hall of Fame along with Babe Ruth's sixtieth home-run bat and other icons essential for proper worship at the altar in that temple of the national pastime. I often imagine Abner Doubleday, surrounded on high by the likes of Grover Cleveland Alexander, Lou Gehrig, Jimmy Foxx, Babe Ruth, Honus Wagner, and maybe today, Satchel Paige, congratulating his fellow Cooperstonian on this sterling contribution to the history of the Game—the "Ball."

Chapter 2
Aviation Enthusiast and the Tin Goose

The Great Waldo Pepper, another movie triumph for Robert Redford, was fifty years in the future when I was growing up in the 1920s; yet it brought back vivid memories of my childhood. LaFleur Field, on the edge of the Berkshires, had a romantic ring to it, as though it were a small field just behind the lines from which the brave Americans of the Lafayette Escadrille took to the air to challenge the Red Baron during that late, great war. Barnstormers frequently came to Northampton, but the closest I ever came to seeing them was from my backyard as they towed long banners while making their noisy passage across the sleepy little college town, Sometimes they would shower us with handbills, making LaFleur for that day the center of my universe. No amount of nagging, pleading, praying had any influence in my quest to see the brave men in their flying machines come to earth on that magic turf.

My desire evoked even more strident pleas after Lindbergh's flight and landing amidst cheers at Le Bourget. Even Dad seemed enthused by the feat of the Lone Eagle. I remember his heavy-handed adjustment of the three tuning knobs on the Stromberg-Carlson in the living room as he pursued his usual frenetic search for the words of Floyd Gibbons and what then passed as the evening news. "By God, he made it!" came forth, interspaced between the loud squawks from Marconi's poorly refined contraption. That event seemed to be a breakthrough in my quest to visit LaFleur and see and smell one of those great red, blue, and white birds that daily awakened our neighborhood. I think Dad (who saw himself as a futurist) caught the significance of Lindy's feat and developed a newfound interest in flying. In any event, a few months later he called down from his third-floor study, "Bo, would you like to go flying in a Ford Trimotor?"

This invitation seemed unreal, but energized me to bolt up the two flights of stairs to confront him face to face. Was it true? Yes it was, but what is a Ford Trimotor? I was always full of questions, and I always received an answer. When I was seven, doubt never clouded my faith in what I heard. "Old Henry Ford turns them out in his factory between his 'tin lizzies.'" I was too young to pick up the sarcasm that was invariable when Dad referred to any car other than a Hupmobile; by then he was the proud owner of his third. His reply, however, brought on another question: "Does that mean it is made of tin?" He replied, "Yes, and that's why they call it the 'Tin Goose.' Now go downstairs until dinner, and I'll tell you more about it then."

An invitation to leave, while given kindly, was not to be ignored, so I ran down to excite my mother with word of Dad's promise to take me flying in a tin goose. I was greeted with a reserved, "Yes, your father and I discussed it last night after he read the ad in the evening paper. I hope he knows what he's getting into. I don't know how safe it is, and anyway he'll never hear the end of your nagging now." I hardly heard her words, and her lack of enthusiasm did nothing to dilute my excitement and visions of going off into the sky in a great bird of tin.

The day of the big adventure came a week later; my excitement had been at its zenith since the enterprising crew of the trimotor had flown leisurely over town one afternoon, towing the flapping banner announcing rides at LaFleur every thirty minutes. Lindbergh, awaiting clear weather at Floyd Bennett Field a rainy morning in 1927, could not have been more anxious for the dawn to arrive nor would he have gleaned less sleep in the passing night. The Lord smiled on us, and the dawn arrived clear and calm. I catapulted out of bed, bolted down the hall to Dad and Mom's room, and broke ground, landing on their bed in a much unappreciated intrusion. Dad was awake. Although I was unaware of it at the time, I am sure he was more than a little concerned about what apocalyptic fate might be his reward for making such an impulsive promise.

I arrived at LaFleur sitting next to Dad who was driving his well-polished Hupmobile Century Eight. There it stood, flashing bright sunbeams from its silvery skin—the biggest plane I had ever seen or imagined: The Tin Goose! The eager hangers-on were standing about and gawking. In the middle of the crowd were two tall, handsome young men, one sporting a rakish moustache in the fashion of Colonel Roscoe Turner, my second hero after Lindbergh and soon to be winner of the Cleveland air races. Both men had well-polished brown leather helmets with

The Tin Goose

tinted goggles pulled high over their foreheads. Only now, as I recall the scene, do I wonder why the helmets and goggles were necessary to pilot a plane with an enclosed cabin. However, at the time, I am sure I would have been disappointed to see my heroes bareheaded and obviously inappropriately attired for their role as pilots. It was only at the end of the flight that I was aware of the brown leather jackets and the white scarves loosely tucked around their necks.

We worked ourselves rapidly through the small crowd as I held Dad's hand and led the charge. Dad identified us to the taller of the pilots, and we were ushered aboard, entering the plane from the rear. Because we were first, we were seated just behind the pilots' door; my eager face was pressed to the window. The wicker seats had cushions and were fastened to the floor. There were arms for the fearful to grasp. However, there were no belts to remind the timid of impending disaster. Soon the cabin was filled with excited youngsters and terror-stricken fathers, trying heroically to maintain the demeanor appropriate to a Sunday commute to Springfield on the Boston and Maine. After what seemed a millennium, the pilots dispersed the crowd. They then ascended the aisle to the pilots' cabin in a manner appropriate to a president-elect approaching the dais to be sworn into office by the Chief Justice of the Supreme Court. Without a word to the great "unwashed" sitting anxiously in the wicker chairs, they closed the door to the inner sanctum with all the authority commensurate with their station. After due deliberation the motors were started, one by one, in an awesome display of power, accented with noise and vast clouds of black dust.

We taxied slowly to the south end of the sod strip that was LaFleur's main and only runway, adequate for Jennys and other barnstorming biplanes of the era but an anachronism in the age of flight being ushered in by the Trimotor. However, none of this was my concern as the roar of the three motors, invading the unsoundproofed cabin, fueled my excitement as I pressed my nose more firmly against the window. Slowly the Goose slid along the green strip and gained speed as the frame grunted and groaned; the wicker chairs squeaked and cracked, and the whole plane vibrated and lurched like a jeep on a washboard road. Suddenly the roar of the motors reached a crescendo, the lurching ceased, and we seemed to be transported into another realm as we left the ground behind like an unwanted chain.

The noise in the cabin was much too overwhelming to allow for talking, even screaming, let alone more subtle forms of communication. I can recall, even today, the great gasps of relief from the adults who were, en masse, questioning their sanity during that mad dash down the sod runway toward certain destruction. I was too busy imprinting the window with the marks of my nose and cheeks to be aware of Dad's reaction to this thrilling flirtation with death, but I do recall his complaining to mother about painful wrists later that day. In retrospect, his bear-grip on the wicker armrests was the most likely cause.

The announced 15 minutes in the air seemed to pass in seconds, but the view of that beautiful New England college town, set in the foothills of the Berkshires, left a mark on my memory that still remains. The scene often returns to me as I seek a restful refuge in my mind's eye from the rush of worries that so often descend on one in the course of a busy day. The sudden bump, repeated twice, as we touched down and bounced briefly back into the air, was followed immediately by a return of the groans of the frame and the squeaks of the seats, to be drowned out by the gunning of the motors, as we taxied back along the soggy grass runway.

When the motors were cut and the plane came to an abrupt halt, I became aware of Dad. He was suddenly in the enthused and ebullient state that I came to associate with his assessment of great accomplishments at times in his life. His immediate comment was "That was great, Bo. We'll have to do it again." I know now he was probably saying to himself, "Jesus Christ, that was close! Never again!" But his countenance radiated the same gleam captured in the front-page pictures of Lindbergh's face as he waved to the French crowd at Le Bourget in his hour of greatest triumph. Seated securely behind the wheel of his Hupp Century Eight, leaving behind the memories of LaFleur Field and his recent encounter with the Angel of the Lord, he hummed quietly to himself one of his favorite hymns from his childhood: "I'm saved! Saved! This is my story: Jesus my Savior cleanses and keeps me . . ."

And although the promised re-run never happened, the Day of Days at LaFleur has impacted my life for sixty years. It still colors my excitement as a private pilot, as a passenger packed like an anchovy in a commuter jet, as a wartime aircraft engineer, and even today as an observer of a young woman in an old Piper crop-duster towing a glider aloft into the blue sky above the Arizona desert.

Chapter 3
Dreams of Glory

The New Yorker magazine of my youth frequently featured a cartoon depicting a young boy ("Small Fry"), deep in the accomplishment of some gargantuan task. He might be confronting Hitler, man to man, with both guns drawn, or slaughtering a man-eating shark with a short hunting knife, while in a swirling stream of blood. Much like that youth, I had my own dreams of glory that were occasioned by the various stimuli that excite a ten- or twelve-year-old. Certainly some of my imaginary exploits were inspired by Dad's storytelling and accounts of his life and times. I suspect that his adventures were further embellished in my own memory. Many were of hunting and fishing adventures: great feats in the field and with a rod in a mountain stream.

Few of those, however, outlasted the early years of youth. Some may have been extinguished by one episode that still haunts me.

We spent a cold late November night in our cabin on the edge of the Berkshires, anticipating the noon opening of the deer season. Great tales of bucks with championship racks that had fallen to the tracking talent and deadly accuracy of Dad and his friends excited the fantasies of this twelve-year-old. I listen to these wizened veterans as they blended cigar and pipe smoke with the last sparks from the dying embers at the back of the old Franklin stove. Looking back, I wonder why I was included in the unique admixture of plumbers, carpenters, and intellectuals from the Smith College faculty that Dad had so characteristically assembled. All were held together by the male bonding of the hunt. I suspect that he, suffering from a sudden attack of parental guilt, had decided that I should be introduced to one of the rituals of male passage. I vaguely remember a not-uncharacteristic outburst: "Goddammit, Grace, I learned to shoot a shotgun when I was half his age." In the face of such overwhelming evidence, she had apparently acquiesced, and I was included in the trip.

The next day I was assigned to follow closely behind Dad, helping him carry the necessary equipment for an afternoon of reclining on a deerwatch. We were dusted by a thin fall of autumn snow, spiced with a 20° norther. Had I been older, I might have been warmed by the haunting nostalgia of lines of a Robert

Frost poem. However, at twelve, I had not yet that literary educa-tion and was only energized by the fantasies of a large buck bursting through the pines and white birches in a flurry of snow to be felled by Dad's double-barreled Parker 10-gauge, loaded with double-0 buckshot.

I was suddenly roused from a cold-induced leth-argy by the appearance of what I recall as a gigantic 12-point buck, lazily nosing the partially snow-cov-ered browse, as he came into full view from among the pines, not 100 feet from our watch. What hap-pened next should have been repressed into the deeper structures of my cortex: Dad stood up slowly, took deliberate aim, and then remained frozen like a tableau in a wax museum. Now I understood what one of the nimrods had laughed about in front of the fire the night before, describing his brother-in-law: "The bastard just froze. Buck fever." And they all laughed. (The brother-in-law was also said to have been all "clapped up," one of several unfathomable conditions I heard of for the first time that night.) Af-ter what may have been a couple of minutes, the big buck slowly exited into a dense clump of white birches, still nosing the browse.

Slowly, Dad lowered his magnificent 10-gauge and looked down at a bewildered twelve-year-old who had been expectantly waiting for a twin burst of double-0 buckshot and heard only the rustling of the pines. I gingerly asked if what had happened was "buck fever" or being "clapped up." Just what directions I was given is uncertain today, but they involved some warnings of dire corporal consequences if anything further was mentioned to anyone concerning this aborted execution of Bambie's grandfather. In some ways, I think he was secretly relieved. Years later, as I hunted in the fields with him, his deadly aim on such man-eaters as cottontails, quail, and pheasants was a source of justifiable accolades. How-

The great birdshooter afield

ever, stories of the glory of the Great White Hunter seem to lose their luster.

Aside from ventures in field and stream, accounts of contacts with some of my heroes of those and later years still echo in my memory. Unverifiable though they may have been, they were the bricks and mortar from which my dreams of glory were formed. What boy in the 1930s wouldn't have been inspired to fanciful reveries when his father, returning from a lecture tour in Texas, noted that he had traveled all day by Pullman across the state with Melvin Purvis, exchanging tales of the "Lady in Red," John Dillinger and the G-men? And how Melvin Purvis and J. Edgar Hoover unleased a barrage from their submachine guns and cut Dillinger down before he could escape in his souped-up Model A? Or stories of accompanying two of his summer students on forays on campus at Cornell when they were the original Durango Kid and Franchot Tone? And then there was the account of his kindness to the aged in giving up his lower berth to William Jennings Bryan, who at the last moment could book only an upper berth.

Tales were legion of drinking bouts at the Round Table at the Algonquin with H. L. Mencken, George Jean Nathan, Sinclair Lewis, and Theodore Dreiser and of dinners at the Lake Shore Club in Chicago with Clarence Darrow, discussing the sorry state of liberalism in the Bible Belt, and of a feast with the deposed Kaiser Wilhelm at Haus Dorn, disputing who started the world war. And then there were debates with Norman Thomas on whither the New Deal and with well-known clerics on whether we had reached the twilight of Christianity. There were the phone calls coming in on our party line when we lived in rural upstate New York from Floyd Gibbons, Lowell Thomas, Will Rogers, Roy Howard, Charles Lindbergh, and the like. After one of these calls Dad would remark, "That'll give the nosy old bitches something to talk about." And on and on.

And so, as I grew up, the dreams became less those of a father, the Great Hunter, and more of him as a mover and shaker, a man who traveled among the well-known intelligentsia of the age. I began to see him as a cru-sader, a leader of causes (whether for justice for Billings and Mooney, Sacco and Vanzetti, and, later, Caryl Chessman), and as an evangelist for prison reform. Even today, when I take the ferry across San Francisco Bay, I am reminded of his role in the successful efforts to close Alcatraz as a wasteful anachronism.

Yet, with all the shift in my visions of him and the dreams of glory they elicited, there still remain some from the mind of the young boy, continuing to picture his father as the mighty, the strong, the invincible be-ing, the primal hunter. A sudden sadness enveloped me one day when we were fishing together on one of those large, public boats that put off from the docks into the rolling Pacific tide. He seemed to fight not to lose his balance in the mild ocean roll. Suddenly he was old and fragile and seventy-eight. No longer the

Frank Buck of Big Game Hunters, the Jack Dempsey of maulers, the Jim Londos of Madison Square Garden. A world was passing rapidly before my eyes, and I was feeling alone and strangely vulnerable.

Chapter 4
Master Host, Bathtub Gin, and Memories of the Volstead Era

There was a loud shout, half amazement and half anguish, as Dad came slamming upstairs to his office. "Jean, look at this goddamn check for $5.00. It's a year's royalties on *Prohibition versus Civilization*.[1] I'm going to frame it and hang it over the bar." For most authors, drawing their living from book royalties, such a check for a year's sales would have been devastating, but as I look back on it, he seemed to view the book as a tract, a vehicle for venting his spleen about the eighteenth amendment, the Volstead Act, and "rot-gut liquor." Actually there was little evidence of a drought in the Barnes household. Prohibition even created an opportunity for Dad to display his proclivities as a host, installing the trappings of an oasis in the arid, boozeless desert of Northampton, the home of "Silent Cal," our law-abiding president and an avid teetotaler. For Dad, Prohibition was, in the words of his fellow journalist Will Rogers, "better than no booze at all."

Bathtub gin is remembered as a myth of the 1920s, but in our house it was a reality. Dad may have been a frustrated engineer, a stymied doctor, but he was certainly not a thwarted apothecary, at least when it came to mixing various assorted herbal and other flavors with grain alcohol. Our Italian immigrant vegetable man, with his one-horse wagon that always sported an umbrella to protect him from the sun and an occasional summer shower, was our unlikely bootlegger. Although of the same heritage as Al Capone, he lacked the class, associates, and connections of Chicago's Own. Rather than supplying imported scotch, gin, and Canadian rye, he limited himself to 5-gallon cans of grain alcohol that he tucked beneath onions, beets, and ears of corn. This raw material fit the needs of the Great Pharmacist, who loved the challenge of blending and bottling his own products. I recall seeing Dad, upon his return from trips to New York, Boston, and elsewhere, unloading his briefcase filled with miniature bottles of flavorings, each a diminutive replica of the genuine pre-Prohibition product.

The next day, or prior to any large gathering at the Barnes oasis, great mixing and bottling began. The flavorings included bourbon, scotch, gin, and Canadian and Pennsylvania rye, along with an assort-

ment of exotic liquors, many of which would be unknown to me even today. The solvent in greatest demand, probably because the 1920s were at the height
of the martini era, was gin. In any event, gin was
pushed by the Great Pharmacist when he turned Bartender and Host. This inclination may have been
partly related to his realization that the essence of the
juniper, mixed with grain alcohol, was the most palat-
able of his liquors. It may also have been his life-long
fixation on the concept that the host is always judged
by the rapidity with which his guests achieve a level
of surgical anesthesia. In any event, gin was the one
liquor that was indeed mixed in the upstairs bathtub,
carefully taste-tested by the Pharmacist, and then
ladled into an assortment of well-worn yet distin-
guished bottles bearing fine labels, such as House of
Lords, Bombay, Tangueray, and the like. The less-
popular liquors were appropriately mixed in dish-
pans and various cooking receptacles, depending on
the expected demand. All were carefully taste-tested
by the Master before being funneled into the collection of bottles that branded them to be of the finest
pre-Volstead stock. I once asked Dad where he had
acquired his priceless bottle collection, but I never received an adequate answer. My suspicion is that the
gathering of these took place just before Prohibition
and consumed a significant amount of his time and
talent as a bargain-hunter. In any event, the Barnes
household of the late 1920s and early 1930s was
stocked with an assortment of well-filled glassware

that would have done justice to the best speakeasy on Chicago's South Side.

Love of the martini may have originated with Prohibition and bathtub gin, but its aficionados have clearly changed their preparatory procedures through the decades. I remember spying down from between the rungs of the upstairs railing and viewing the Host rhythmically agitating a large German silver cocktail shaker filled with the volatile mixture. At the same time he attempted to keep in some cadence with the soporific crooning of Maurice Chevalier that emanated from the Victrola horn on which was pictured the little white terrier. It was a method of preparation far removed from that advocated by today's martini habitués, who can be seen pouring the liquids carefully into a glass pitcher, stirring cautiously with a glass rod, all to avoid "bruising" the precious contents. How different from the neolithic rites of the 1920s! And today, if drunk at all, the martini is imbibed in fashionable lounges and quiet restaurants, and its consumption is hardly accompanied by the frenetic gyrations of mini-skirted flappers executing the Charleston.

Dad was, in all things, democratic, and he never limited his profligate distribution of liquor and wine to any particular class of visitor of friend. He was certain, however, in all things, including matters of taste, what individuals should like and what was best for them. For his farmer friends and the day laborers who worked on the farm where we lived during the last days of Prohibition, he had a one-two sequence that seemed to offer a welcome respite from the day's drudgery and, to some, a knock-out punch. The lucky, or hapless, souls, depending on one's view of "demon rum," invariably left the back door belching a happy song of praise to the Lord of the Manor as they staggered down the highroad to town.

Number one in the sequence was a derivative of hard cider. The farm had an abundance of apple trees that yielded a goodly harvest of apples, some half rotten; but as Dad insisted, "They'll add the flavor good cider needs." These were taken to a local cider mill and the resulting juice poured into hogsheads in the basement. To this was added molasses, honey, brown sugar, and raisins, and then the entire mixture was allowed to ferment for a month or more. From this evolved two additional products: the first was apple "champagne," developed by placing grain sugar in the bottom of a wine bottle, filling it with the actively fermenting cider, and sealing it with a cork and tape. The result was pronounced as being "better that anything Louis Quatorze ever swilled down at Versailles." The other product was the number one punch in the first salvo delivered to outside workers. It was produced from the hard cider, after maximum fermentation and with the help of one of upstate's 20° below zero nights. The cider was placed outside in a pail or other suitable receptacle, whereupon much of the water was frozen and lifted from the remainder, leaving what was called applejack, a drink of significantly higher proof.

The second punch (reputed to be 120 proof) was delivered from a well-worn bottle impressively designated in Gothic German with the pious label of Kirschwasser. The vessel must have been bottomless; it was poured from almost daily in generous proportions and was never seen to be refilled. As he dispensed the Kirschwasser, Dad invariably recited the saga of the bottle—a personal gift from Kaiser Wilhelm at Haus Dorn in 1927. The tale was embellished: it was indeed a treasure the Kaiser would usually share only with his most valued compatriots! Dad's presentation was so well delivered that I still have childhood visions of "Kaiser Bill" in full uniform and on horseback, sporting a steel helmet, which was topped with a spire. Equipped with a large saber hanging from his belt, he would be bending over to bestow this bottle of Kirschwasser on his esteemed friend, my Dad.

Our farm had significant rows of Concord grapes, excellent for table use and appropriate for making Passover wine for holidays but hardly the grape to produce a classic varietal. However, this did not deter Dad, who now, almost like a "Christian Brother," took up the robes of a Master Vinter. Miraculously, the bottle collection was expanded to include well-stained but authentically labeled items denoting an origin from some of the outstanding estates of the Loire Valley, Burgundy, and similar prime Gallic vineyards. Peaches and plums were also in abundance on the farm, and they, in turn, were pressed fermented, and bottled under the vinter's meticulous supervision. Because these prime products were only brought out for state dinners attended by sophisticates from New York City and other major world centers, I have little memory of their reception. However, I would assume that the guests' tastes and judgments had been so anesthetized by the pre-meal libations that Mogen David would have readily passed as a full-bodied Burgundy.

The noble experiment passed into history in 1933 with Repeal, but the reservoir of grain alcohol–based liquor, hard-cider derivatives, and concord grape varietals continued to furnish libation at the Barnes farm for a number of years. In retrospect, Dad and Jean must have had a coterie of loyal friends and fans to have withstood these continued assaults from the remnants of the Volstead Era. When Dad moved to the California coast in the late 1950s, his bargain-hunting instincts again surfaced, and guests were presented with Ernest and Julio's finest from the old Gallo wineries in the same well-used French bottleware. What goes around, comes around!

Chapter 5
Hasenpfeffer Maven

"Jean, your goddamned friend, George Knippus, is going to be here this weekend, and he'll want hasenpfeffer." This was said as he poured them each a before-dinner martini made with bathtub gin left from the recently deceased noble experiment—Prohibition. (Despite being well-to-do by Depression-era standards, Dad retained many of the frugal habits of an upstate farmer and seldom threw anything away, even the relative lethal concoctions of the Volstead days.) The use of the Lord's name in damnation translated into a seal of approval of George as a special and close friend of the family, not just an acquaintance. The "your friend" was added to guard against any disagreement from Jean as to the weekend arrangements, which were, undoubtedly,

made by Dad in the first place. George's family
moniker was really Knipp, so the designation of him
as Knippus was a further affirmation of close friend-
ship. I learned early the special meaning of certain
words and expressions and that they often denoted
sentiments other than those that appeared on the surface, a valuable preschool experience for a future
psychiatrist!

Jean's enthusiasm for hasenpfeffer was limited,
but she was a good sport and knew that George
would take over the major preparation in any event.
Dad had a tone of enthusiasm in his voice as he anticipated the challenge of securing the rabbits to be pep-
pered (and vinegared) for this Germanic feast. It
meant a day's reprieve from his usually tightly disci-
plined hours of exhausting work at his desk, grinding
out more editorials, book reviews, pages of intellectual history, and replying in his own pungent vernacular to the letters of dozens of correspondents.
These included ex-students and poor, misguided
"boobs" who had the audacity to disagree with the
"Liberal Viewpoint," his daily Scripps-Howard editorial. And since we had moved back to an upstate
farm, close by the old family homestead, the quest of
the hasen presented the heart-warming opportunity
to recapture his youth as he walked the fields and
fencerows of his early years.

The only person genuinely distressed by the pros-
pects of a rabbit hunt was me—not that the thought of
a day in the fields with my father was in itself dis-

The fruits of a great rabbit hunt of days long gone

agreeable. Quite the contrary. Even though it might not be a colorful dash over the countryside with horse and hounds, it could be an invigorating experience, particularly listening to Dad's vivid and exciting yarns of the great hunts of days long gone by. It was Dad's new method of rabbit-hunting that sapped my enthusiasm for the projected activities of the morrow. Traditionally, we would go out with one or two beagles and let them roust out cottontails from the thickets as we waited on each side in ambush— a clean and sporting proposition, at least for the hunters. However, this year rabbits had been on a declining curve and our beagles had been traded for a magnificent basset hound whose previous owner had promised Dad a more effective hunter than "20 damned, baying beagles." We were so struck by the dog's surfeit of facial flesh that hung almost to the ground, along with his elephantine ears, that we immediately named him Rudy because of his strong resemblance to the great crooner Rudy Valley. Unfortunately, Rudy not only could not croon or bay, he also could not track rabbits. He evinced no blood lust deep within his magnificent jowls for the elusive rodents. While on his first hunt, a small bunny running up behind spooked him so badly that he froze in his tracks and shook in fear. Only Dad's pecuniary sense and devious plans for trading him saved poor Rudy from summary execution by firing squad.

Before dawn the next morning, Dad was up preparing his special hunt breakfast: over-fried, slightly carbonized eggs basted with burned bacon grease and multiple slices of Rainbow sandwich bread toasted Texas-style in the greasy remnants of the egg-frying skillet, all washed down with multiple flagons of instant coffee. He made the beverage sweet and syrupy with a lethal mixture of cane sugar and saccharin, the latter a holdover from the austere, sugarless days of World War I. With this load firmly packed in our unwilling but not yet revolting stomachs, Dad and I went to the barn to assemble the equipment for the Great Rabbit Hunt, sans dogs. In this era of rabbit infertility, Dad's new and secret weapon was a pair of "domesticated" ferrets, which in those days could be ordered from any number of ferret farms that advertised in various hunting journals. Domesticated members of the weasel family, ferrets were generally unfriendly to man and loved to eat rodents, particularly plump cottontails. The trick was to find an active rabbit hole and send the ferret on its mission in the hope that the rabbit would hear the marauder and exit in panic from the backdoor, to be unceremoniously shot by the sportsman. There were several drawbacks, however, one being the natural hostility of the ferret to other mammals, including the higher apes. To handle this problem was easy, although tricky: open the ferret box, grab him decisively behind the head with a heavy pair of leather gloves and thrust him headfirst into a tightly secured leather bag. The bag was stored in the back of the hunting coat, unless the hunter was overwhelmed with a sudden wave of castration anxiety in which case he would carry the bag in plain view along with his gun.

Another problem was that the weasel-like stealth of the ferret might lead to his successfully stalking the rabbit in his hutch and then taking a half-day long postprandial snooze before exiting. This left the sportsman with the alternative of waiting the rest of the day, or night, on a windswept, snowy field to reclaim his property or to let friend ferret return to nature. And the final problem facing us that day had to do with the legality of hunting with ferrets. Due to the downturn in the rabbit population, sportsmen's

groups had convinced the legislature that using ferrets for hunting purposes should be prohibited.
"Meat hunters," such as Dad, and an odd assortment
of staunch defenders of personal liberty made a last-
ditch and futile attempt to head this legislation off,
but the "damn Democrats" from downstate carried
the day and ferrets were emancipated from bondage,
except for those owned by a few recalcitrant defenders of the rights of private property. Dad's concerns
with this issue were more pragmatic and not in the
least philosophical—how to have rabbit for hasenpfeffer! So with a bit of profanity he dismissed the
danger of the game warden—"Too cold for the bastard to be up and around"—bagged our two reluctant
hunting partners and off we went. He obviously felt
confident and secure as he stowed the bag in the back
of his hunting coat.

It was a miserably cold, cloudy day with a frosty
haze already settled over the snow-laden fields and
fencerows. The old Model A started with a cough and
sputter and was obviously ready to go, appearing to
laugh at the two expensive Hupmobiles, which would
never start on a morning like this, and the Rolls Royce
newcomer that had arrived in late summer from
someone's Wall Street bankruptcy and had promptly
hibernated. We ended up going across the main high-
way, up the dirt road, by the old family homestead,
and finally parked in the school yard of the country
school where both my grandfather and my dad had

taught. Due to the urgency of the quest for the hasen and the frigidity of the dawn, I was spared the recital of historical minutiae that this old building usually brought forth: like how one-room schools at the turn of the century, even in the advanced commonwealth of New York, were fortunate to find teachers with a high school education, and so on. I often envisioned Dad, a big, awkward boy, just out of twelfth grade, teaching eight grades of farm children. Inevitably, the oldest of these were more interested in upsetting their recent peer (who was trying to maintain some semblance of order) than in learning the rudiments of English grammar. What practical experience this must have been for a boy who would someday sit in class with the father of progressive education, John Dewey! However, by his own testimony, Dad's method of discipline at that pre-enlightened time in his career was far from progressive and strictly hickory stick. He boasted with almost sadistic pleasure of his vigorous adherence to it.

The leaden December sky was just showing a faint band of crimson to the east as we climbed out of the Model A, pulled our guns out of the back seat, and started down a hedgerow leading from the school yard toward the next farm. The 2 inches of new snow crunched in the subzero cold with a high pitched squeak under each bootfall. Dad broke the silence for the first time since leaving home. "We're in luck, Bo. The tracks should be fresh and going right into any of the good holes. We'll have more damn rabbits than old Knippus can eat in a month." He crunched on ahead like a Zulu warrior tracking a fast-moving cheeta, leaving me struggling ten paces behind—not an unusual formation for our hunts.

I had just settled into as fast a semi-trot as the early hour allowed when I heard a loud greeting up ahead. "Jesus, Bo, come look at this. It's like a whole tribe of rabbits gathered for Wednesday night prayer meeting." With this he reached into the game pocket of his hunting coat and pulled out the ferret bag. With very little ado, but with a staunch leather glove guarding his hand, he pulled the male ferret from the bag and pushed its nose unceremoniously into the opening of the rabbit hole. "Alright, you big bastard, roust them out." In his haste to get into the morning's work, he had committed the cardinal sin of such a hunt: He hadn't located the other end of the hutch. At the point I was just bringing this oversight to his attention, there was a loud rustling along the fencerow as a half-dozen rabbits ran helter-skelter in all directions. By the time we recovered sufficiently to play the traditional role of executioners, the victims had fled the scene, oblivious to our ceremonious but ineffectual 4-barrel departing salute. Mr. Ferret must have been equally surprised with this sudden exit as he popped his head out of the backdoor outlet and set off in his characteristic lopping gait in hot but futile pursuit. Dad caught him by the neck and thrust him back into the darkness of his bag with an angry denunciation: "You're too goddamned fast, you hungry son of a bitch."

The ferret interlude served to delay the long burst of profanity that I knew was about to erupt. To my surprise the reaction, when it did come, was relatively mild; accusations of guilt (such as, "Why in the hell were you way back there?") were largely omitted. Actually the words that began to emerge were foreshortened by the unexpected appearance of Dad's old hunting partner Dave Douglas, coming toward us on the other side of the fence. Dave owned a farm beyond ours and across the outlet, and he had the same primal hunting instinct as Dad, that insatiable urge to produce, whether rabbits, birds, or deer. Dave appropriately commiserated with Dad on our recent misfortune, shared a swig of Calvert Reserve from his flask with his old hunting buddy, and suggested that we join forces to see that "Old Knippus is properly fed."

The day dragged endlessly on, the sky grew more leaden and occasional light flakes of snow further emphasized winter's death grip on the upstate terrain. My memories of the remainder of the day are vague, probably erased by the inevitable fatigue of trying to match the pace of these two obstinate meat hunters, driven by genes of unnumbered generations of men who worked the soil and hunted God's bounty in the field for family sustenance and surcease from their grinding labor. Mr. Ferret was in and out of holes all day and became so obviously tired and unenthusiastic about his appointed duties that we escaped the

catastrophe of his catching Brer Rabbit in his hutch
and bedding down for a long sleep. By the time the
pink glow had settled slowly below the western horizon and the cold had further confirmed its control
over nature, we too gave up. "By God, Knippus will
have his goddamned hasenpfeffer" was Dad's benediction to a day in the field, a benediction washed
down with the last drop of Dave's Calvert Reserve.
And Mr. Ferret and I, as kindred souls, joined in a
silent prayer of thanksgiving.

Chapter 6
Cats and Dogs and
the Rural Mentality

The screen door of the kitchen slammed behind me as I bolted out in response to the increasing drone of an airplane motor. Simultaneously, I was aware of a red biplane tugging a long advertising banner and my dog Buster's loud yip of pain. Before I had time to read the message flapping behind the plane's tail, I heard a loud scream from my mother; "You cut off Buster's tail, and he's splattering blood all over my kitchen." With that she let out a distress cry to my father to come down from his third-floor office and take care of the mess. Dad and I arrived back in the kitchen almost simultaneously, just in time for me to hear his "For Christ sake, Grace, what the hell is going on here?"

As it turned out Buster had been following closely behind as I rushed out the kitchen door, and the tip of his tail was cut off cleanly as the door slammed shut. Although Buster may have been immediately shocked by a burst of pain, by the time the three of us surveyed the blood-splattered kitchen, Buster was more excited than injured and demonstrated his forgiving nature by continuing to festoon the beige trim of the kitchen with bright, crimson splotches of beagle blood. I was immediately commanded, "Bob, get your goddamned mutt out of here and keep him out." The fresh hemoglobin washed off cleanly, and the only residue of this episode was the tip of Buster's tail, which seemed to show up for months at odd moments in our backyard.

This scene seems appropriate for introducing the reader to the domestic animals that played an important role in our family life and illustrates Dad's rural attitude toward cats and dogs, an attitude that changed in interesting ways as he aged.

On the Old Family Homestead, where Dad grew up, dogs slept on the front porch in the summer and in the barn in the winter but were never welcome in the house. They were fed table scraps, hunks of meat left over after a pig or cow was butchered, and milk at milking time, as were the cats. They were used as watchdogs and to help herd the cows in from the pasture at milking time. If a farmer had leisure time for rabbit- or bird-hunting, an appropriate beagle or setter occupied a special place in the dog hierarchy in the rural canine realm. However, such baronial status did not include house privileges.

Cats were ubiquitous and generally resident in the barn, corncrib, and various sheds stretching out beyond the back door. Occasionally, my grandmother would take a liking to a particularly promising black female who would sneak into the kitchen, rub against her legs, and jump into her lap, purring and looking up at her with the eyes of a vamp. All cats (whether residents of barn, shed, or house) had a major and valuable function on the farm—rodent control. A good mouser was expected to provide much of her own food, although evening milking time always brought cats and milk together in the barn. It was a meeting place and time for all cats. Unfortunately cats seemed governed by Malthusian principles and periodically their numbers outgrew the rodent population and the farmer's generosity. This situation turned them into foragers and avid hunters in the fields surrounding the farm. It placed them in direct competition for rabbits, quail, and pheasants with those bucolic nimrods bent on broadening their leisure activities by stealing a few hours in the fall from the grinding work routine of the farm. Interestingly, Dad and his grandfather were the only Barneses exhibiting such a bent; Dad's father and two brothers had less than no interest in autumn forays into the fields.

The consequence of this perceived competition between man and cat was often disastrous for the unfortunate feline who roved the fields ostensibly in search of bunnies and feathered bounty, which the farmer now visualized as festooning his Thanksgiving table, midst pumpkins and cranberry sauce. Execution was readily justified by reference to overpopulation and "saving the little rabbits," not to mention the nesting quail and baby pheasants. Such acts, while serving the higher purpose of salvation for these precious little beings, were seldom discussed at home; they passed as quiet murders, unsolved by any prying gumshoe.

Buster, of the lost tail-tip, was our first house dog and was tolerated by Dad out of deference to our then urban life and the idea that "a boy should have a dog." He also rationalized that Buster was a beagle and thus "a rabbit dog," who had at least some smidgin of utility. Years later my stepmother, Jean, acquired a brace of rare midget pointers and insisted that they be house dogs. Dad acquiesced, noting that they were pointers and, thus, potential bird hunters. He promptly named them Voltman and Dianne, as though descended from the canines of some mythologic Teutonic court. Their residence in the household was relatively brief, however, because they seemed to feel their noble lineage entitled them to eat from the master's table.

Their final performance came during the war when Voltman grabbed a newly broiled filet from the edge of the stove and rushed out the door. Such cuts were rare and valued in the war years, and this one had been particularly hoarded in honor of my sister's current boyfriend and his introduction to the Barnes house-hold. Dad, who entered the kitchen just as Voltman exited, noted the empty plate on the stove edge and immediately assessed the culinary disaster about to be consummated. A loud bellow issued from the kitchen as he reached for the shotgun that routinely sat by the kitchen door and exited directly behind the pointer. Jean entered the kitchen and, sizing up the situation, grabbed a broom and went noisily after Dad to protect her beloved Voltman. The filet was saved, washed off, and served; Voltman was not executed; and the boyfriend never returned. However, this episode ended both the housing of dogs in the Barnes house and the introduction of new boyfriends.

The change in Dad's attitude toward cats displayed another facet of his character: a sensitivity and concern for life balanced against the harder patterns inherited from his youth, separated as it was by less than a century from the harsh realities of the American frontier. I was home from college on the Christmas weekend of Pearl Harbor December, a frigid, snow-burdened holiday. Returning from snowshoeing and savoring the thought of a hot whiskey sling, I was rushing to the back door when I caught the movement of a white object on the hill in front of the winter house. After taking the snowshoes off, I went upstairs to Dad's office and mentioned this to him. A break in the monotony of his afternoon of proofreading, with Wagner in the background

interspersed with Milton Cross's comments, produced a sudden surge of adrenaline. "Bo, hand me
those field glasses." The command was followed in a
moment by a loud "Jesus Christ, it's a goddamned
bobcat!" From his selection of rifles, prominently displayed directly behind his desk, he grabbed his prize
Winchester .405, proudly described to all who visited
as "the same rifle that Teddy Roosevelt used to kill
elephants on his famous African safari in 1902." The
upstairs window was thrown open, and this action
was followed in a few moments by an ear-breaking
"vroom" from the gun designed to stop a charging
grizzly 2 feet from the petrified hunter. Watching
through the field glasses, I reported a light dusting of
snow emanating from a patch of ground just above
the white object's head. Dad seemed pleased by the
report and was probably silently relieved that he had
not demolished the poor feline. His only remark was
"The poor bastard deserves to live!"

Some two hours later, with the blast from Teddy
Roosevelt's rifle still ringing in my ears, I heard what
seemed to be a scratching on the kitchen door. I
opened it to reveal a magnificent white Manx cat with
a bobbed tail, looking up with plaintive eyes. Dad's
response was totally unexpected. He reached down
and affectionately picked up the cat, carried him
along to the kitchen cabinet where he selected a cereal
dish, took it to the refrigerator, and poured out a large
portion of milk. He then put the cat and the milk
down together, petting the cat's head and letting out a

The big, white Manx cat awaiting its warm simian greetings

soft but audible "There kitty, kitty." It was as though some memory trace from his childhood had suddenly been activated. From then on, as long as Dad and Jean lived in Cooperstown, the big, white Manx cat was in and out of the house on his own schedule, accompanied by soothing simian purrs from Dad, "Nice kitty, kitty." Incredible! From intruder deserving of the Teddy Roosevelt .405 treatment to beloved pussy!

The affection for cats grew even deeper when Dad and Jean retired to Malibu, where a black Siamese named My Sin and a tiger-colored mate, Mr. Cat, teamed up as the household idols and staunch rattlesnake hunters, proudly dragging in their prey for affectionate praise. One day Mr. Cat apparently moved too slowly and was never found but was appropriately memorialized by a small, marble headstone overlooking the broad expanse of the Pacific and Catalina Island. God in his infinite wisdom does indeed work his wonders in strange ways!

Chapter 7
Hupmobile Man

"He's a damned Democrat" was the way my grandfather characterized a business acquaintance from Auburn. In that part of upstate, Democrats were few and far between in the late 1920s. When Grandfather was growing up, after the Civil War, political affiliations were often the means of personal classification. Today, yuppies' children earmark adults by their profession and thus, not too subtly, rank them on the socioeconomic ladder: "My old man's a plastic surgeon," and sotto voce, "He makes more than your dad who is only a CPA." In the 1920s, when I was growing up, men were classified by the cars they drove and their long-term loyalty to a particular make. My cousin Lee's father always bought Packards and was thus a Packard Man. My uncle

Fred was a Studebaker Man and our old family friend George Knipp, a Buick Man. And in our circle of friends there were Reo Men, Hudson Men, and an occasional Essex Man. The latter had the misfortune to be renamed by us small fry with a moniker suggesting that he was afflicted with a perennial gluteal discomfort.

Today it would be difficult to imagine referring to a man or woman as a Mitsubishi Woman or a Toyota Man, and the designation of someone as a Rolls Royce Person would seem to be in unconscionable poor taste. But in the 1920s Dad was four square behind being referred to as a Hupmobile Man,* and after a couple of birdbath martinis made with the finest gin, direct from the bathtub, he would loudly proclaim the virtues of that marvel of human locomotion. His hyperbole would have given embarrassment to the ad writers describing the vehicle in the slick pages of *Judge* and the old *Life*. When asked, "What's your old man?" it would never have occurred to me to cast him as a professor or writer. "Oh, he's a Hupp Man" was my unfaltering response. So deep was his fixation on being a Hupmobile Man that I recall him claiming,

---

*Hupmobiles were produced by Robert and Louis Hupp in Detroit between 1908 and 1941. They were medium-priced cars, well regarded and popular in the 1920s. The final models, produced in the late 1940s, were radically aerodynamic for the time, and included the product of the corporate acquisition of Cord, the Hupcord.

The Hupmobile Man initiates his son to the world of the Hupp

after two of the birdbath concoctions, that Hoover had meant to proclaim, "A Hupp in every garage and a chicken in every pot," but that Henry Ford had dissuaded him at the last moment with a large campaign contribution.

Beginning in 1922 and ending sometime just before the war we had six different Hupps. My earliest memories involved Dad's first Hupmobile, an open soft-top with isinglass side curtains that snapped on for cold weather or rain and gave some semblance of protection. This car was proudly named the Green Goddess. I was much too young to remember how it functioned in the cold winters of the Berkshire foothills, without a heater, defroster, and all the modern necessities of motoring. It was replaced by the 1928 Century Eight, proclaimed in a full-page spread in

Robert H. Barnes

The first Hupp—the Green Goddess

Judge to "usher in a new era in motoring." This car was Dad's pride and joy and was kept waxed and polished at all times, an uncharacteristic state considering Dad's rural background and the proverbial antipathy of farmers to routine maintain-ence chores. The car, however, had a very special place in his heart, and years later he had an enlarged photo of the Century Eight, with himself standing by the front fender, pinned on the wall next to his typewriter. I was much too young to consider ever driving this magnificent vehicle, but I do remember sitting on Dad's lap, trying to steer it down the back street near our home. My small hands could hardly turn the large wooden steering wheel. Power steering was, of course, several decades in the future.

The 1928 Century Eight Hupmobile

Four years after the Century Eight was sold, Dad bought his largest and most elegant Hupp: Robert and Louis Hupp's attempt to stem the financial onslaught of the Depression—a magnificent steel box on wheels with a gas-devouring, 133-horsepower, straight-eight power plant. It had an interior of chrome and veneered wood that was reminiscent of the decor of the Empire State Building of the same era. Its top speed was a secret but was said to be "over a hundred." "Barney Oldfield would sure like to get his hands on this baby" was Dad's response to the top-speed issue. All my growing-up years I had heard of the great Berna Eli Oldfield, known to his fans as Barney. According to Dad, the great repository of historical facts, Mr. Oldfield was the first man to be clocked at "a mile a minute" in Henry Ford's famous 999 racer. So it seemed only natural that as we were returning from one of Dad's frequent trips to Auburn, 9 miles to the south of our farm, there would suddenly develop a new burst of activity from the 133 horses under the hood. Dad demonstrated a certain anxious alertness as he gripped the great mahogany steering wheel. His knuckles began to shine with the clear whiteness of well-polished ivory. "Hang on, boys, we're going to open her up!" We leaned forward in an intense excitement, half aware that the roadside trees and the old Burma Shave signs were passing more rapidly than usual. All our eyes were focused on the speedometer. I watched it slowly pass 70, then 75, and on to 80, before finally coming to rest at 84 mph!

Slowly Dad relaxed, moved back from the wheel, and loosened his grip on eternity, so that a reassuring redness returned to his knuckles. "Well, she really moves" was his only comment as he regained his equanimity and attempted to make little of his accomplishment, quite as though it were the usual order of business driving back from Auburn. We were full of comments and appropriate awe, and by the time our old barn, festooned with the mammoth CHEW MAILPOUCH sign came into view, we had covered all the comparisons with the Indianapolis 500, Barney Oldfield, Ralph DePalma, and a half-dozen now forgotten names of that ancient racing fraternity. Life moves on—today any delivery boy in his half-wrecked Toyota pickup would exceed our appalling pace delivering a pizza down an unpatrolled residential street after midnight.

Unfortunately the Big Hupp fell into more and more disuse as the Depression era gave way to the excitment of the prewar days and the draft. Summers and warm weather months were soon over in upstate New York, and the 6-volt batteries of those days were of little avail in turning over the great 133-horses when frosty mornings descended on us soon after Labor Day. The cold seldom left before the graves were flag-draped for Decoration Day. Before Dad accepted this annual reality, much commotion and references to the Lord and His Son were accompanied by pouring teakettles of boiling water over those 133 horses, always to no avail. The basic family transportation was provided by an old Model A Ford coupe with rumble seat. For those in the front, a primitive airscoop over the block brought a few precious calories from the warming engine, which usually began to heat after the first 20 miles. Later, the coupe was replaced by a Model A pickup that had been retired by the telephone company after 200,000 vigorous miles; it was repainted bright crimson and repeatedly pronounced "the best goddamned vehicle old Henry ever made." My memory fails as I try to recount the final fate of the Big Hupp, but its 6-miles-per-gallon appetite for fuel further doomed it as gas stamps joined sugar rationing, late trains, boot camps,and basic training in the early 1940s.

We did have two more Hupps before dealers and replacement parts became extinct, but they seemed more like ordinary cars, not Chariots of Distinction. In the Barnes family they were soon replaced by a string of Dodges and Fords. And so passed an era of my childhood. Dad no longer retained the status of a "Hupmobile Man," sinking instead to the demoted rank of "writer."

Chapter 8
Bargains Galore

Anafranil, the trade name of a new drug that has made one of America's wealthy pharmaceutical companies even wealthier, is used to treat obsessive compulsive disorders, the agonizing disability that forces the sufferer to wash his hands every time he touches a doorknob or to retrace her path, making sure she did not run over an innocent pedestrian at the last crosswalk. My compulsions are minimal, but somewhere along the way I picked up the habit of turning over my cup to read the name on the bottom every time I go into a restaurant. Is it Syracuse China? I am not sure whether I am more at ease to find it is or is not, but I have an irresistible urge to find out. I never dared tell my analyst about this compulsion. After all, there are some things one does not tell the silent listener at the head of the couch. In any event, I thought he preferred to hear dreams of libidinal cravings and the guilt they evoked. Besides, analysis can cure guilt but not compulsions, and my cup-turning activities were not disabling and certainly did not merit the investment of a $25-hour. (Yes, this was many decades ago, before the $25-hour went out with the 5-cent cigar and the 10-cent hamburger at the White Tower.) And today this compulsion continues to be a lesser menace than the side effects of the new "wonder drug."

Many blame their life-long quirks on their parents! And so it is with me. Dad was an inveterate addict of bargains, whether at auctions, sheriff's sales, or manufacturers' outlets for "seconds and defective merchandise," including Syracuse China. So many painful, boring, tiring, and embarrassing hours were unavoidably spent, without hope of rescue, as a helpless participant in such endeavors. Maybe I developed the cup-turning compulsion as a defense against any expression of anger from a dutiful son on being so drafted. Because I rejected the $25 investment, I will never be certain.

Invariably, on the way home from a boring trip to Syracuse 25 long miles away, we made an unwelcome detour to the Syracuse China Company Outlet Store (for damaged and discontinued tableware). At that time, and even today (if the Koreans have not usurped its place), Syracuse China was the major producer of dishes for the type of restaurants that line the main tourist routes through and between our great cities as well as Chinese eateries, lunch counters, and any establishments wishing to protect their inventory from chipping or inadvertent slippage into open handbags. Such misadventures were deterred by the heft and thickness of the sturdy Syracuse design.

After what always seemed like a 2-hour wait, Dad would struggle toward the car with a huge box of what inevitably turned out to be mismatched, often chipped, and occasionally cracked soup tureens, sugar bowls, platters, egg cups, and gravy pitchers with their firmly attached dripping dishes. Also salvaged were salt and pepper shakers, ashtrays picturing the 1933 Chicago World's Fair, and assorted coffee mugs. Had he just been awarded a Nobel Prize, his look of pleasure and satisfaction could not have been greater.

Such detours occurred at least quarterly for about ten years, and the accumulated treasury of stored ceramics would have lined the 25 miles between the Syracuse China Company and our farm with an alabaster display worthy of Forest Lawn. These treasures furnished tableware for our many camps that came and went through the years and provided replacements for the high mortality experienced in Jean's ceramic stores from the dishwashing chores, for which we children were so inevitably drafted.

Closely related to searching for bargains in mismatched tableware was the quest for silver-plated table settings and other dining room metallic implements and receptacles. The Oneida Community was famous in upstate New York for its heritage of "Bible Communists" and non-monogamous marital arrangements. Although these reputed activities passed into history by the 1880s, the memories lingered on with the natives, which included our family. The rest of the world knew of the community for its Oneida Silver, and Dad knew of it because of its outlet store for discontinued and defective silver plate. We made fewer stops there than at Syracuse China, but undoubtedly the purchases were more expensive. To me they were less offensive, however, because I could look up at the houses and imagine orgies being consummated even as I watched. Visits also occasioned many questions about sexual habits and practices—my own pre-Kinsey survey. To this day, stored in garages and attic recesses in Barnes-related homes, there are boxes filled with a variety of patterns— sugar bowls, cake servers, candy and nut plates, and other equally useful items, all in the style of the 1920s and bleeding the underlying copper through the retreating silver.

Of all the bargain hunting expeditions, the one episode that most affected me personally occurred in 1933, when I was twelve. At that time we had moved to the farm in upstate New York, just 3 miles south of Port Byron where both my father and mother had gone to school. Dad daily visited the Port Byron Main Street, which could well have been placed on the old MGM lot as a setting for *State Fair, Oklahoma, The*

Music Man, or some other bucolic reminder of America's small-town heritage. On one of his forays to deposit mail and pick up some Sen-Sen and other necessities at the drug store owned by his friend Earl Blake, Dad's attention was directed across the street to a sale at Art Blauvelt's Haberdashery. To compare it with Harry Truman's fabled men's store of the same vintage in Kansas City would have been like measuring it against Bloomingdales; but Art made up in friendliness what his emporium lacked in size, inventory, and style. He greeted his old classmate Harry with all the enthusiasm a used car salesman lavishes on his first customer of a weekend morning.

On this memorable day, Art was featuring an all-out, sellout of stock acquired during the last year of World War I: stove-pipe pants and multi-pocket coats, both made of army surplus khaki. In donning the pants, one was required to remove one's shoes lest they became inextricably jammed in the pipe-shaped legs. The coats were ingeniously designed to give a semi-military appearance, attesting to the probability of the customer having answered Uncle Sam's World War I call—I WANT YOU!—even if he had missed it. Whether the marked-down price or the style intrigued Dad is unclear, but his actions were decisive. His judgment dictated the garments were not his style but would be perfect for a twelve-year-old, particularly me. He rushed into the house with a loud, "Bo, get down here. You are old enough to get the hell out of those goddamned knickers and into some men's clothes." So expecting some type of rite of passage into manhood, I readily followed him to the Big Hupp and off we went to Port Byron and Art's haberdashery.

I ended up with two suits, one in the color and texture of the original World War I army surplus khaki cloth and the other dyed an off-color cream. In addition, I was decked out on top with a gray felt fedora that Art assured Dad was a genuine replica of the hat worn by Warren G. Harding at his inauguration in 1921. The suits were tailored, using the term loosely, for full-sized men, not scraggly twelve-year-olds, but Dad seemed assured downsizing was a minor matter and planned to take the goods and myself to Matie Tanner, our elderly neighbor, who specialized in gossip, sugar cookies and apple pies, not tailoring. The final item added to this bargain purchase was a pair of black dancing shoes with long, pointed toes. Art said I wouldn't need to try them on; they would fit fine. Dad, readily agreeing, rejoined that they would look great and that I could "kick some son-of-a-bitch all the way to hell with those toes," a remark that seemed to amuse Art. I vaguely remember some off-hand historical note to the effect that they were the same type of shoe worn by Lincoln the night of his assassination at Ford's Theatre.

I still have a photograph taken of me in a snowstorm, wearing all the accoutrements of this passage into sartorial manhood. Sadly, the pointed shoes are invisibly immersed in snow. I was saved from any further public appearances, thus adorned, when my mother mercifully arrived home from a trip to New York City. The clothes were packed quietly away while Dad's attention was suddenly focused on Roosevelt's bank holiday and other weighty matters such as new bargain opportunities offered by a rash of local bankruptcies.

On one of his frequent 9-mile trips back from Auburn, Dad spied a large, handwritten sign on a bakery, announcing sales of 3-day-old bread, an item of some interest in the dark days of the Great Depression. Shortly afterward, he arrived joyously at home with the back of the car filled with an assortment of white breads in various stages of aging. This was the first of many stops at the bakery, which resulted in a change in diet for our four hunting dogs. The bread was moistened with large quantities of fresh milk, which Dad bought from his brother's nearby farm for 5 cents a quart. This was a blessing for Uncle Seymour, who frequently poured it in the creek rather than take it to the Sheffield Dairy where he was paid 3 cents a quart. "The goddamned dogs live in the world of milk and honey" was Dad's frequent response to this new bargain food. A number of months after the initiation of this diet, we noted that the dogs began to have occasional episodes of running for several minutes in concentric circles before collapsing. This behavior continued for a number of months and then mysteriously stopped, At first it was amusing, and Dad suggested it was some kind of sexual frenzy.

However, I was greatly relieved when it stopped. At about that time the bakery went into bankruptcy and the dogs regressed from their bargain heaven of milk and honey to more conventional meals of Purina Chow. Only years later, when I was in medical school, did I stumble on an article concerning running fits in dogs, reportedly caused by agenized flour, which was prepared with a chemical universally used for bleaching white flour. Dad rejected this explanation, sticking to his theory of sexual frenzy and insisting that milk and bread was "God's own diet for dogs." Besides it had been a wonderful bargain!

Of all his stops on the lecture circuit, his favorite was Cleveland. Not only was he welcomed by the local gentry and his talks favorably reported by the *Plain Dealer*, but he also had the opportunity to stay at the home of his long-time friend, Joe Newman. Joe was a delightful conversationalist and a well-informed host. He and his brother owned a large and well-stocked sporting goods store. Knowing of Harry's love of bargains, they always arranged a very special sale when he was in town, and invariably Dad left Cleveland happy and laden with various useful sporting items. One I remember, in particular, because it was awarded to me with great ceremony when I was in high school—a large Spaulding tennis racket said to have been built to order for the great Bill Tilden. I never learned why Tilden rejected it, but I can imagine it was because the large handle was too big for even his mammoth paw. To this day I blame my stunted tennis development on my inability to properly grasp Bill's mighty club.

The purchase Dad was most proud of from his Cleveland connection consisted of two dozen wool, crimson-colored tank tops with bold yellow lettering, proudly announcing the wearer hailed from the house of the St. Ignacias Golden Tornadoes. These were particularly useful shirts when mowing our acres of lawn, weeding the pea patch, and picking cherries in the orchard. Invariably, they would elicit whoops of laughter from passing classmates. Dad's only comment was "They are just jealous of your doing God's work."

Years later I recall expending the remaining Golden Tornado tank top as I polished the last Hupmobile. *Sic transit gloria* . . . and all the other great bargains of my youth.

Chapter 9
Barnyard Caruso

"Read my lips," said the president, and TV viewers spanning three generations were asked to trust in God and the president and believe there would be no new taxes. In the bleak, white Church of Christ, blessed by the Disciples, my dad learned trust from a more personal and non-electronic media: *Triumphant Service Songs*, "compiled and published by Homer A. Rodeheaver, with the assistance of Yumbert and Joseph Rodeheaver."

In the church perched on a lonely, wind-swept hillside, next to a cemetery filled with many generations of Dad's family, Barnes, Storkes, and Shorts, services started promptly at 11:15 on each and every Sunday morning and regularly on Wednesday evening at 7:15. Raw-boned, callous-handed, red-

The Church of the Disciples

faced farmers, dressed in their ill-fitting Sears woolens, gave forth with great, sonorous bursts of Christian theology. Each family cluster included a dutiful and weary-looking wife and an abundant brood of clear-eyed, energetic, and impatient "young-uns." The entire service was directed and controlled by a sweating, aged but energetic matron, exuding an aura of bucolic piety quite in keeping with the ancient organ she so vigorously pumped with both feet. At the same time, she pushed and pulled the stops above the keyboard in a valiant but vain attempt to add further tonal depth to the Rodeheaver collection.

"Only Trust Him," "Trusting Jesus," "Trust and Obey," "Blessed Assurance," and "God Will Take Care of You" were but a few of the messages of trust that were etched in the minds of the more serious youths. No need to "read my lips" to develop a trust in the eyes of the beholder or the ears of the auditor. But I suspect that Dad's consciousness was more imprinted with the strong but discordant notes of a booming base, a proud tenor, or a slightly squeaky soprano emanating from the assembled chorus of vociferous Christians.

From either these indoctrinations into fundamentalist Christian liturgical music or his later introduction to the opera and the great Enrico Caruso at the Met when he was a young graduate student in New York, Dad developed a deep and clamorous fixation on vocal renditions. He regarded himself as gifted, with the potential of becoming a consummate vocal interpreter. This fixation, whether ambition or hope, was amusing although often annoying to others because his proficiency in carrying a tune was comparable to that of bullfrog bursting forth on a moonlit night. In later years, when he became somewhat rotund, he would often compare his girth to that of Caruso and indicate it was related to their mutually inherent pneumatic gifts.

Had he been Jewish, Harry would undoubtedly have considered a career as a cantor, ready to bring his liturgical talents into the life of the synagogue rather than wasting them on the bare walls of his family's Campbellite church, hard by the cemetery on the hill. As I remember from my youth, the only remnant of this great but lost talent appeared on Saturday afternoons when the deep, saccharin voice of Milton Cross slithered forth from one of Dad's studies, followed by Lauritz Melchior's booming tenor, or the overwhelming zeal of a Wagnerian diva. Then, if it were one of his favorite Puccini operas, a gusty, off-key rendition would originate from the noted author.

Dearest to Dad's heart, however, were the old, fundamentalist hymns of his youth. Whenever anyone with only the most elementary talent as a pianist dropped by for a visit, including one of our rural mail carriers, an invitation would immediately be issued to all nearby to join in glorious and pious intonations to the Father, Son, and Holy Ghost. Some of my fondest memories of family affairs involved these joyous gatherings around the piano; each participant was supplied with a copy of the Rodeheaver, *Triumphant Service Songs*, a pile of which was kept in constant readiness for just such impromptu events. Dad generally assumed the right to pick the selection, even if the poor pianist had never heard the hymn and could hardly read music. An exception was made when my grandfather was there, and then he had the privilege of picking the first offering. With Grandfather it was always, *"Little Brown Church in the Wildwood."* His big, booming voice would intone *"Come, Come, Come"* ad infinitum as the rest of us carried the words of the hymn. After that, Dad again made the selections. He invariably favored those carrying such colorful confessions as, "*I Need Thee Every Hour,*" "*I Was Lost in Sin,*" "*I Love to Tell the Story,*" "*Let the Lower Lights Be Burning.*" Occasionally another member of the circle might be permitted a selection or the pianist herself might insert, "*In the Garden*" or commit the ultimate sacrilege of resurrecting a non-liturgical selection such as "*Irish Eyes.*" Then a silence settled over the room and the group evaporated. The unsuspecting pianist was not invited again and also was not offered an opportunity to imbibe of the host's liquid dividend for good behavior.

To this day, on a warm summer's evening, I can still hear my father's voice, notably off-key, intoning the opening lines of the "Railroad Man's Hymn": "Jesus Christ is my conductor, never falter, never fail, keep your hand upon the throttle and your eye upon the rail . . ." And I can visualize the faraway look in his mother's eyes as she caught a glimpse of the Savior snatching her favorite son's soul from the Devil.

Chapter 10
The Learned
Curmudgeon: Epistles
from the Old Underwood
How to Alienate
the Great Unwashed

Dad was among that band of notable critics of early twentieth-century American society whose vivid and often raucous observations reached their zenith in the 1920s and 1930s. H. L. Mencken, editor of the *American Mercury*, and certainly the most caustic and influential curmudgeon of that era, frequently corresponded with Dad and sometimes published Dad's iconoclastic barrages. They often met at the Round Table in the Algonquin, along with other literati of the day—George Jean Nathan, Sinclair Lewis, Upton Sinclair, Theodore Dreiser, and the like. Dad and Mencken were undoubtedly the most prolific of the group and the most corrosive in flailing "boobus americanus."

A crusader for a large array of causes, Dad launched his verbal missiles at a wide variety of targets. Toned-down salvos were frequent in his published volumes and even in his academic works. Acidic bombardments were often found in his daily columns in the *New York World-Telegram* during his glory days with Scripps-Howard in the 1930s. However, his major fusillades were showered on those who ruffled his feathers by disagreeing with his strong beliefs. And most of his beliefs were strongly held indeed! Relatively few close to him totally escaped such treatment, although it was often somewhat softened by an attempt at heavy-handed humor. However, woe to the public figure whose pronouncements conflicted with one of his crusades. Special missives were dispatched to that errant "boob," either by mail or via a letter to the editor.

Because of Dad's long-standing interest in crime, prisons, and civil liberties, he often became deeply involved in campaigns to save the principals in such notable cases as Billings and Moony, Sacco and Vanzetti, and more recently, Caryl Chessman. Edmund Brown, then governor of California, was advised to "deal with the Chessman case in the same statesman-like manner with which you have already courageously handled many important and difficult problems in your duties as Governor."[1] Unfortunately this counsel was not heeded and Chessman succumbed in the gas chamber. This led to a follow-up reprimand: "Inasmuch as I sincerely believe you to be a decent and kindly man, apart from your political techniques and ambitions, and since I know you are fully aware that you did not state the truth when you said that the evidence of Chessman's guilt is 'overwhelming,' I believe that Chessman's future may well be more enviable than yours. . . . I believe that you will awake in a cold sweat many nights after facing Chessman's ghost in your dreams before you are 'gathered in' to join him and Judge Fricke in the 'Great Beyond.'"[2]

A letter to an old acquaintance who had suggested a certain reviewer for one of Dad's new volumes contains an excellent example of his command of forceful invective, not unusual when a review was not highly favorable: "I don't know why you had to turn to one of the most malicious, superficial and pompous asses in the entire academic and literary world."[3]

His evaluation of the Republican occupants of the White House in the 1920s and early 1930s was hardly more charitable. Coolidge was described as a man whose "personal traits are of the type which appeal with unparalleled force to the Babbitry, Gopher Prairieism and peasantry of this country which make up more than ninety-five percent of our population."[4] Hoover received similar treatment as "one who has no warmth in his being save for the predatory pirates who have wasted and squandered our national heritage and will ultimately turn us over to Fascists, revolutionists, or both."[5]

Those residing comfortably in academia often received similar treatment, particularly if their niche was within a history department. "All history which does not bring better understanding of the problem and does not offer some solutions may be regarded as 'bunk.'"[6] This pronouncement was followed by the observation that the average college professor was a "pathetic person" with "distilled water on the brain."[7] The entire enterprise of higher education received special analysis.

> Closely associated with the punitive ideal is the solemnity-complex which dominates conventional pedagogy. The whole teaching process is assumed to be a gloomy and earnest affair. Light-hearted enthusiasm is wholly out of place here. It is in as bad taste as a horse-laugh at a funeral. Hence, it is not surprising that there is little life and vitality in contemporary education. Akin to this is the notion of academic dignity, partly an outgrowth of the solemnity complex and partly a defense of teachers against embarrassing questions and intellectual familiarity from students.[8]

Parents did not escape his scathing comments as to their involvement in the educational enterprise. "Education, as the average parent conceives of it, is subsidiary and accessory to the custodial objective. It is designed to make young people more amenable to segregation while inmates in an educational institution and to make them docile and well-regimented citizens when their school and college days are over."[9]

Organized religion received especially vehement consideration (as one would expect from a reformed fundamentalist). "It is the thesis of the writer that the orthodox religious complex is, in its multifarious ramifications, the most active and pervasive menace which confronts mankind today, compared with which war and poverty are unimportant, incidental details."[10] The Judeo-Christian theology was further singled out for lengthy treatment in *The Twilight of Christianity*: "For two thousand years millions upon millions . . . worshiped, sacrificed, and martyred themselves for a deity who had sprung from the imagination of this small tribe."[11]

In 1932, he completed a 128-page tract for Viking Press entitled *Prohibition Versus Civilization*.[12] In it the Curmudgeon assigned much of the blame for foisting the Great Experiment on the American people to the philosophical stance of Christianity.

> The underlying philosophy of Prohibition is a direct outgrowth of the otherworldly perspective of Christianity. This point of view assesses all earthly customs, habits, and indulgences solely with reference to their direct bearing on salvation in the world to come. Anything that promotes earthly happiness and leads to forgetfulness of salvation is adjudged evil, wicked and a fatal threat to the well-being of the race. Worldly joys and comforts are reprehensible and undesirable. The validity of a social goal or an individual habit must be judged solely in reference to salvation in the future life.[13]

As the years passed from the boom days of the 1920s to the depression decade of the 1930s, issues changed, but the invective that rolled forth from the platen of the old Underwood never faltered nor did its colorful hyperbole fade. Unfortunately, at the end of Dad's *World-Telegram* era, the general public was more and more denied access to the thoughts of the Learned Curmudgeon. However, those of us close to him and his wide circle of friends and acquaintances were blessed with an increasing volume of personal messages, which were never diminished in their content of colorful and insightful vituperation. A gigantic storehouse of these messages remains simmering in the American Heritage Center archives in Laramie, Wyoming.

Putting aside all the hyperbole and iconoclastic overkill in the vast volume of his published works and much of his personal correspondence, one must continually be impressed by his deep insight in matters of public policy and personal and civic cupidity and hypocrisy. Few men of his time had the educational background, the vast reservoir of energy, and the sheer brain power to comprehend and expose so wide a world view of society, its heroes and its charlatans, and its ever-changing and often confusing directions. He was a futurist of the first magnitude, and his commentaries and predictions ring ever more true when retrospectively viewed from the lofty perspective of the last decade of the millennium. One can only wonder what the old Underwood would have brought forth had it been kept busy in the years that have passed since its sudden consignment to the dustheap on August 25, 1968.

Chapter 11
Dad as a Mentor
How I Grew Up
and Became a Doctor

"Harry, it's time for Bob to start school. He's already five and school opens next month." And thus my mom opened a new chapter in my life. Dad, busy thinking of something else, replied, "Sure, Grace, anything you want, go ahead and do it." His attention was undoubtedly on the welfare of Sacco and Vanzetti or the vivid accounts of one of the Dempsey-Tunney imbroglios and the long count. In any event, he obviously didn't hear what Mom was saying. Being from that "old school," hearing about a five-year-old starting school would have reminded him of his first days in a one-room schoolhouse where all the kids from grade 1 through 8 sat in the same room and learned their As through Zs, accentuated by the frequent tune of the hickory stick. Had he listened, his response would have been, "Fine, Grace, get him registered in the brick schoolhouse down the hill." The big, old building was down in the factory district below our house. It always scared me when Mom and I would walk by it around Halloween. At dusk it seemed to smell of the dead and of black bats, and I once thought I saw a snowy white, vaporous figure float from an upstairs window.

Mom had other ideas and quietly registered me to start first grade in what I soon learned was the Smith College Day School, a small, cozy building located on the college campus. Here the Smith girls learned teaching skills just in case they didn't marry a future stockbroker from Princeton or Yale. (Remember, this was the era of *The Great Gatsby*.)

A few days later it dawned on Dad what Mom had done. There was a loud discussion in the kitchen. All I heard, as Dad slammed out of the kitchen, was Mom saying, "But Harry, it will be easy for you to leave Bob off in the morning on your way to meet your classes." I don't remember anything further being said, other than a loud "Humph!" from Dad as the kitchen door swung closed.

When summer was over, there was great stir as Mom gathered me up to shop for new shirts, matching shorts, and knickers, which would be needed when the weather became cold as it soon would in the foothills of the Berkshires. Then, suddenly, the time was at hand, and I started the first of those never-ending days of school. Little did I know of the years and years of September starts of new school years that were beginning on that first day. If I had known, what would I have done? I was only five and didn't comprehend what even one day was like, let alone the 7,000 or more that lay below the horizon of the future!

Smith College Day School was a wonderful experience for a five-year-old; the clean, fresh-smelling classrooms, filled with flowers, were attended to by attractive, perfumed, bob-haired, 20-year-olds, eager to learn from observing well-behaved faculty children supposedly exhibiting refined and demure behavior and possessed of superior intelligence. The educational philosophy was laissez-faire and early Dewey progressive. No pressure to learn the three Rs. Free play and self-expression and attention! Oh that attention—how could a young boy not grow up loving beautiful young women!

Too soon the serpent slithered into this Garden, tempting the children with the apple of hedonism— fun and games, the love of attention, and no rote lessons in reading, writing, and arithmetic. Suddenly on a February evening Dad was struck with an unexpected burst of family interest and tarried an extra five minutes at the table after dinner. My educational attainments were the focus of his interest, and before Mom could divert it to other areas, he handed me the front page of the *Springfield Republican* and asked me to read the headlines. The written word, whether English or Sanskrit, was not part of the first-grade Dewey curriculum, at least not at Smith College Day

My forceful mentor

School in 1927. I am not sure exactly what happened at this point, but I do remember some very pointed comparisons being made: "Jesus Christ, Grace, when I was four I was reading *Innocents Abroad* by kerosene lamp on the floor. This is the first and last year of that goddamn progressive education. I want him in public school, even if he has to repeat the first grade." And so I was cast out of the Garden and thrown to the mercy of public education and into the first grade again for yet another year. I was to learn much more of the smelly old brick school in the industrial area below our house. The punishment for this original sin was harsh indeed, and even time on the analyst's couch years later failed to erase the hurt and shame. Such was my first experience with mentoring at my father's knee!

School changes were frequent over the next twelve years (there were eight different schools in all), but the memory of that next September and the shame of repeating the first year linger, along with the odor of floor-cleaning compound, uriniferous scents in the halls, and creaky stairs. Then there was the scowling, overweight matron, worn down by thirty years of tending 40-plus undisciplined first graders and repeating the attendance roll, morning after morning. I did learn that all teachers are not young, beautiful, and perfumed, and although I never read *Innocents Abroad*, I did master the alphabet, spelling, and the multiplication tables. I also learned about fire drills, spitballs, fights in the school yard, visits to the principal's office, and other activities that were not part of progressive education at Smith College Day School. In retrospect, Dad's first effort at mentoring did better prepare me for the real world, much as the exit from the Garden prepared mankind for survival in a bleak, pietistic universe.

The less frenetic college days of fifty years ago allowed for time between semesters, and I used the period after my sophomore year to make some career decisions. Having recently been enthused by James Burnham's popular monograph on the managerial revolution, Dad had decided I should pursue a social science line and become a governmental manager, much akin to those known today by the Washington pundits as Beltway bureaucrats. I had rather passively accepted this decision until I realized such a course brought me into constant contact with Dad's numerous academic fields. Being the son of a household name may have been reassuring, but it was hardly a status that boosted one's ego: "Oh, you're Harry Elmer Barnes's son," and on and on. The need to be one's own man and many other influences led my summer soul-searching to a firm decision to become a physician. Making that decision was easier, however, than announcing it to my forceful family mentor, who was a person of strong and often unyielding conviction.

I can remember the aura of anxiety and even panic that surrounded me as I climbed the stairs to Dad's second-floor office, timing my entrance to coincide with the fading lines of *Aïda*, which was soon followed by the tranquilizing Saturday afternoon exit benediction from Milton Cross. This background promised to add an even more mellow ambience to a soft, Indian summer day and to cushion expected paternal explosion. He was sitting with a pipe in his mouth, a proofreader's visor shading his eyes from the last rays of sun setting over Jimmy Allen's hayfield, facing an emerging document about to be cast out by the old Underwood with the double bars on top. He momentarily stopped his rapid, two-finger hunt-and-peck pace on the well-worn keyboard, the one with the green rubber caps, and pushed back his typing chair. I was welcomed in with a warm "Come on in, Bo," his sign of affection, which seemed to reduce my panic. At that, he reached down and pulled the about-to-be-born masterpiece from the aged and hardened platen of the Underwood. "Here, read this. Old Mencken will get a kick out of it." At that point, I was sorely tempted to forget the purpose of my painful pilgrimage up the stairs and pass a jovial ten minutes before we both retreated downstairs for the serious business of Saturday afternoon cocktails. Somewhere a quiet voice spoke up within: "If you are ever going to be a doctor, you've got to do it." With that I put the letter to H. L. to one side and began a slow, stuttering "Dad, I've been thinking . . ." And so it slowly unfolded.

He sat there, pushed back from the old Underwood, with his eyeshade slightly recessed on his forehead. He listen intently, fixing me firmly in an unmoving gaze, neither friendly nor unfriendly, but intent. Not eliciting the explosion I had anticipated, my voice strengthened and my pace accelerated. He glanced down at his pipe that had lain unused in a large ashtray beside the typewriter, picked it up, packed down the cold, half-burned ashes, and lit the remnants. A foul-smelling white cloud, sprinkled with small particles of what could have been volcanic ash erupted briefly, as though ignited in response to some evil and seditious forces, deep within the bowels of the earth. No sooner had the cloud deposited its whitish dust over the old Underwood than it abruptly withdrew from whence it had come, almost as suddenly as it had arisen. No vigorous inhalations resuscitated it from its sudden demise. With that, Dad replaced it deliberately in its previous resting place, slowly took off the green visor, and pushed back his chair. "Let's go downstairs so we can have a drink before Jean puts on dinner." My anxiety returned as I noted, almost subliminally, that I was not invited as Bo or even Bob.

The lack of an outburst should not have surprised me. Dad was not given to acrimonious face-to-face confrontations, even with his son. Drinks and dinner were filled with more than the usual periods of silence, but action on the Russian front and in the Pacific were discussed, for indeed the summer of 1942 was full of fateful news. Nothing further was said about my new career plans, college, or medical school. The three of us sat for a few minutes enjoying the dying embers in the fireplace when Dad announced he was going to bed. Jean followed him soon afterward, while I stayed behind to clean up the dining room and kitchen, my assignment on weekends at home. From my bedroom I could hear Dad expressing strong opinions on some subject, interspersed with calming responses from Jean. The words were indistinct but the emotions driving them were not lost. I knew that when I returned to college after the weekend, the words and emotions would no longer be indistinct but would come by mail, ejected with vehemence from the old Underwood with the double bars on top. Harry Elmer Barnes, author, journalist, publicist, was master of the English language—one who, when aroused, poured out acrid volleys of type guaranteed to inflame the viscera of more volatile recipients to a near-homicidal frenzy or completely demolish the tender egos of more sensitive souls.

After fifty years, much is forgotten of the contents of that single-spaced, two-page letter, which started with"Bob" and ended abruptly with "HEB." Somewhere near the beginning was a personal observation: "I'd rather see you be a goddamned plumber or carpenter than a doctor." Toward the end came the permission I had sought: "If you want to be a goddamned fool, go ahead." Other than a brief wave of guilt—"I've let him down"—which rapidly passed, I was greatly relieved and proceeded home that next weekend. The first evening home, at one of the interminable round of Cooperstown cocktail parties, he put his arm around my shoulder as he introduced me to a new recruit to the cocktail circle. "This is my son, Bob. I've advised him to do something serious for humanity and go into medicine. He'll be a real 'doctor,' not one of these bogus ones, like me."

Chapter 12
Dad as a Role Model
Further Thoughts on
Learning by Example

Dad was not your typical father, even judged by the changing standards for the archetypal male parent that evolved during the Roaring '20s, the '30s of the Great Depression, and the war years of the '40s. But in my memory, he was a good father and, in many ways, even an exemplary one. Because he did much of his writing at home for many of the years I was growing up, he was available for my interminable questions about all areas of life. This conditioned my deep faith in him and the veracity of every pronouncement he might deliver, no matter how extreme: "I'd trust Al Capone a hell of a lot further than that SOB." (The name of a prominent politician, a leading banker, college president, or publisher could be substituted as years passed and disappointments and frustrations grew.) As a result, I began to believe the world was inhabited by devils, perhaps an occasional saint, and a vast number of Mencken's "boobs."

I learned very early what were the appropriate athletic and recreational activities—hunting, fishing, baseball, and an occasional trip to the movies. Golf was for degenerate country-club Babbits and hardly a source of significant exercise or physical challenge, even in those days before the now-compulsory golf cart. The game was never viewed as a business opportunity or a valued social occasion, particularly since women were seldom involved. Tennis was worthy of watching but probably not with any frequency if you were a busy person, unless, of course, Bill Tilden was in town. Certainly, boxing and wrestling were more than acceptable male sports for spectator enjoyment, particularly in the days of Dempsey, Tunney, Strangler Lewis, Gus Sonnenberg, and Jim Londos. Later, I learned that dancing was a suitable activity for men but primarily for the mild libidinal gratification it offered. It should be viewed only as an opportunity for close contact with an attractive woman, not as a valued accomplishment of artistic merit, unless, of course, performed by professionals on stage or screen. Cocktail parties were to be lauded for offering stimulating interchange with attractive persons, usually of the opposite gender. They might be a focus for fruitful social "small talk" but hardly a place for significant intellectual exchange. Almost all athletic and recreational events were to be given secondary importance to productive efforts, with the possible exception of the World Series, championship boxing matches, and cocktail parties as a reward for a twelve-hour day of labor.

Dad was very much a man of action, not openly introspective but given, in a John Wayne sense, to "shooting from the hip." Orders were issued and strong opinions expressed as to what I needed to be doing. "While you're home over Christmas, you might stack up that wood over in the orchard"—even though it was 10° below zero and there were probably 50 cords covered with ice and snow. (This type of activity seemed quite natural to him because he would have been expected to do it without question when he was ten, at least according to the mythology he so readily broadcast on appropriate occasions.) Once, out of frustration with my mother's complaints that I was always getting my shoes wet in the trout stream in front of our summer cabin, an order was issued: "Stay out of that goddamned brook or I'll whale the hell out of you." However, he was not given to physical punishment, and in the end subsequent infractions were either forgotten or resulted in a clarion call: "Bo, use some time productively and cut the front and back lawn, and then you can go back to fishing."

At the age of thirty-five I took up flying, an event duly noted in an epistle that arrived soon afterward, posing the question: "What is behind this insane death instinct you are pursuing?" Once, after I introduced him to a young nurse I was dating, I received the terse written comment, "She has all the beauty, charm and erudition of a 10-month-old heifer."

Yet it was not these overt orders and expressions of opinion regarding my activities that had a dominant influence on my emotional and behavioral development. Rather it was my observation of his actions, coupled with his vivid and articulate expression of opinions on a wide variety of subjects. For example, *women*. He often proclaimed, in his own unambiguous vernacular, that any sensible man should either pursue intimate activities with women or leave them alone. Although he may have initiated and pursued such activities, he very obviously could never leave them alone. He spent much of his life seeking their company. Subsequently he maintained contact with them for years and decades by letters and visits that included bouquets of flowers. He was never particularly discreet about such activities on his home turf, but the fact that he was never shot, beaten, or otherwise abused by irate husbands, brothers, or boyfriends certainly attests to a degree of self-saving caution or to his readily perceived robust physique.

On the one hand, Dad verbalized an attitude that suggested women were most sensibly seen as sex objects. On the other hand, he held many of those he knew intimately in high regard intellectually and professionally. He also did not look at the world of work as being divided between men's work and women's toil. He was quite capable of washing dishes, cleaning the house, making the beds, and cooking. The culinary activities he pursued with a zest for the basics would have cheered the heart of any Mountain Man of the early Western frontier. He once commented proudly, "Jim Bridger or Kit Carson would have left their 'squaws' alone in their bedrolls to fortify their dawn courage with these fried eggs." Not needing early morning courage, most viewed these greasy creations, speckled by carbonized bacon bits, with a revulsion that was ignored by the Master Chef as he went about adding other culinary creations to their morning largess. Thus, I grew up with a more-than-conventional blurring of roles in the accomplishment of domestic tasks—a lesson that has held me in good stead and has been passed to my children.

Fortified by his phenomenal memory, Dad was loathe ever to abandon contact with a friend or acquaintance. The old Underwood was kept busy on a 12-hour shift, even when Dad was in his late seventies, as he banged out pithy notes to someone out of his past, oftentimes someone whose memory may have already slipped into the abyss of advanced Alzheimer's. He, thereby, maintained a wide network of persons of value to him throughout the world, a network that served him well in the last decades of his life. Keeping contact with friends took a great deal of energy, which he had in vast supply even into his final day. Although a letter from HEB may have brought consternation to the few, certainly to the many, such epistles generated stimulation, a laugh, and even a trip down some long forgotten memory lane. To the recipient, it often brought a renewal of warm memories from an old classmate, an esteemed teacher, or a famous writer. At other times, it served, often in a good-natured way, to keep open some festering memory of a particular disagreement that had rankled the old curmudgeon's viscera. To him, such outgoing messages meant maintaining a grasp on his world, and a wide, wide world it was indeed! Looking back on it today, I better understand his incredible investment of time and energy in the maintenance of his network.

Dad was a master of hyperbole. A restaurant meal, which he alone might fancy or be unwilling to admit was third rate, had to be touted as "better than the Waldorf has to offer." A new but third-rate Robert Hall suit, which I acquired for high school graduation, allowed me to "exude the sartorial elegance of J. P. Morgan." One of our third- or fourth-rate "hunting lodges," smelling of the aging and recycled lumber of an old milking shed, was referred to as "better than Paul Smith's Adirondacks Retreat" (a private resort where the rich and famous of an earlier era—men like Thomas Edison, Henry Ford, and John D. Rockefeller—escaped from the summer heat of the city).

Dad did have a chance to realize one of his exaggerated fantasies in 1932 when he unexpectedly, within four weeks, acquired two Rolls Royces—one bestowed on him by a suddenly bankrupt millionaire who could no longer afford the Manhattan garage rental. The second arrived through similar circumstances but required back garage rental of $500. These were in "mint condition, just off the boat" and were suitably garaged in our barn. The Fourth of July was designated as an appropriate occasion for an introduction of one of these "chariots of the English nobility" to the bucolic upstate scene. The older of the two, a four-door Sports Phaeton (circa 1926 vintage), with a canvas top and clip-on isinglass windows for foul weather, and a motor "as long as the Leviathan" and "ticking like a singer Sewing Machine" was chosen. We were ordered to be prepared to depart by 7 P.M. for our parade to town in order to make our grand entrance just before the fireworks. I recall little of the details of that 4th, but I do remember, as we drove home, Dad singing softly and slightly off-key the words from one of his favorite hymns: "Lord, lift me up and let me stand . . . a higher plane than I have found; Lord, plant my feet on higher ground." The Prodigal Son had indeed returned and in a Rolls Royce! Higher ground, indeed!

For the next several years holidays brought forth one or the other of the Rolls, all gassed, polished, and started. And starting was no mean accomplishment for the 6-volt batteries of those days, particularly considering the Rolls' Leviathan-sized motors. The work of cleaning and polishing, interspersed with loud and recurrent references to the "goddamn incompetent

The prodigal son at the wheel of the Rolls Royce

English engineers," somewhat dampened my enthusiasm for holidays for several years. And then the 1930s passed into the 1940s, and we prepared to move to Cooperstown where that community of "coupon clippers" and "old wealth" would have found little excitement in Dad's holiday RR capers. And so, the Rolls were lost from the Barnes's family, only to live in legend. One was sold to a stockbroker on Wall Street. According to Dad, "The poor son-of-a-bitch jumped out of the thirtieth floor window a week later"; I never verified the tale, but it certainly embellished the legend. The Phaeton was stored in the barn of his old hunting partner, Dave Douglas. Years later the barn and the Phaeton were destroyed in a grass fire—*sic transit gloria mundi*! And so ended the depression and Dad's re-enactment of "The Return of the Prodigal Son."

The Rolls Royce gambol, like so many of Dad's larks, was open to more than one interpretation. Was it indeed a need to show his childhood peers and his father, mother, and brothers that he had indeed made it, even in those tough days of the Great Depression? Or was it another way for him to mock the "idle rich," the "robber barons" and the "economic Royalists"—not an unusual activity for intellectuals and reformers in the 1930s. Probably it was bit of both, mixed in with a degree of envy understandable in a former farmboy possessing some of the same cultural drives and fantasies as his mythical contemporary—the Great Gatsby. In any event, it was another chapter in the saga of living with HEB, one that not only added travail to life but also memories that have worn well with the retelling for over a half-century.

Another aspect of Dad's descriptive hyperbole was his knack for storytelling. Many of his narrative yarns came from his youth, in and around the turn of the century, when rural America was still in the post–Civil War era. In retrospect, some were of whole cloth and some a mixture of fabrication and unverifiable truth. Yet all added to the re-creation in fantasy of an era long passed, giving one the feeling of having been there and lived through that colorful time when America was still young.

One tale, which has come back to me time and again as our environment has deteriorated, painted a picture of the wildlife of his youth. Dad described the carrier pigeons darkening the sky from horizon to horizon as they made one of their migratory moves above the Old Homestead. After Great-grandfather Barnes blasted into this mass with his ancient muzzle-loading, 8-gauge shotgun, primed with black powder and bird shot, Dad and his brothers picked up the birds in bushel baskets. Then, one year, this annual gift from the bountiful land abruptly ceased; it was an omen, unnoticed at the time, that nature, even in America, had its limitations.

Another of his favorite anecdotes came from his high school days. The favorite lunch-time break featured running to the edge of town and dropping down from a low bridge onto the roof of a mule-drawn barge on the old Erie Canal. "We rode like Cleopatra on the Nile to the other side of town and hoisted ourselves onto the last bridge with a wave of good-bye to the amused mule-skinner." Little change had come to the Port Byron of his youth since the canal was dug in the 1820s. That event had signaled the beginning of the great migration that settled the West. The men and women who moved America across the Mississippi and on to the Pacific passed through on that same narrow ditch. The iron horse had long since eclipsed the old mule-drawn canal boats, but this remnant of America's past still remained into Dad's youth—a constant reminder of America's relative youth! This was a reminiscence that added to my perspective of American history and the influence of the frontier on both Dad and myself. This influence undoubtedly resulted in all of us eventually moving West. This perspective has been lost on my children, but they are Westerners, whether or not they know why.

These are a few of the more colorful examples of the manner in which Dad influenced his son's passage into adulthood. The messages were communicated cogently and often in bright, living color. They could not be missed and were well learned, sometimes all too well. In the main I count myself fortunate to have received his unique delivery of these lessons. Surely he did not cast his pearls before swine.

Chapter 13
Bucolic Sanitarian

"Harry's gone mad. I just saw him running around the side of the house with a gun, muttering something about the plumbers." Jean seldom seemed perturbed by Dad's idiosyncracies, but at the moment, she was genuinely upset; so I volunteered to run outside and see what had set him off. As I came around the corner, I was greeted with a very loud gunshot, not your usual .22-caliber ping. I spied Dad, lying on his belly with a rifle aimed at the house, ready to let go another shot. He saw me and held off until I was comfortably below him, and then there was another loud explosion. I realized he was shooting with one of his army rifles into the foundation rock of the house.

I didn't need to ask him for an explanation; it all burst out with a barrage of profanity. "The god-damned plumbers have been chipping away at this wall for two days and charging me plumbers' rates. A hundred rounds of this will take care of it before the bastards bankrupt me." This was followed by a continuing fusillade. I suggested that there might be some danger of a bullet ricocheting off the rocks and hitting him in the head, an outcome he indignantly rejected as he ordered me back into the house to reassure Jean that he knew what he was doing and not to interfere. So the bombardment continued.

An hour later, after the incessant volleys had ceased, a dusty trooper returned from the trenches, looking very pleased with himself but sheepishly admitting that the ringing in his ears was so loud he couldn't hear what was being said. Probably that was a valuable admission, preventing Jean from venting her anger, fueled by a long series of such life-threatening episodes. She had been in favor of an additional wash room in the Stone House but had not reckoned with this re-enactment of the Battle of the Marne: Dad's successful effort to shoot a hole for the drainage pipe through 2 feet of solid stone. Nor had she planned to have a toilet that was an ancient survivor from a hotel demolition, a relic Dad had discovered in a local junk yard. Unbeknownst to her, it was this acquisition that had fueled Dad's interest in suggesting the new facility in the first place. After all, one had to find a use for a bargain!

My sister, Barbara, and I were so intrigued by the ancient throne, which the plumber subsequently installed, that we did research on the origin of the toilet; we learned that toilets with flowing water were first introduced in England by Sir John Crapper in 1709. We created a suitably printed and framed sign that indicated our toilet was indeed Sir John's original product. This seemed to tickle Dad's sense of historical perspective, although I suspect Jean may have been offended by our humorous citation of the eyesore relic.

Years before this episode, we had moved to the country and into a large, old farm house with adequate rooms but only one inside bath. The water was supplied from one of two cisterns and was pumped to an upstairs storage tank by boy power. This made the outside toilet—the outhouse—popular with the younger set, even in the frigid upstate winters. It was a "three-holer," but by accepted usage was never occupied by more than one person. I asked Dad once why farm outhouses usually were three-holers, and he answered that it was to provide adequate seating so the kids wouldn't waste their time waiting and away from their chores. He used this occasion as the jumping-off place to indicate how he had worked as a child from 4 A.M. to 8 P.M., 7 days a week, walked 4 miles to school in the snow, and milked 12 cows twice a day. I once inquired of my grandmother why she and Grandfather had imposed such a spartan regime on their oldest son. She answered with an amused smile, "Just to get him to collect the hens' eggs, your grandpa and I had to roust him away from in front of the stove where he was reading *Life on the Mississippi*, or some such atheistic trash."

Our outhouse was a strong brick building, suitable for a tornado shelter and heated with a kerosene stove that had never been lit. Dad had a wash basin with faucets installed by the door. However, neither the faucets nor the drain were ever connected. I never dared ask why he had these items hung uselessly from the wall, but I inadvertently found out one day when we were expecting visitors from New York. "Bo, clean up the outhouse and make sure the basin is scrubbed, and put this sign on it." He handed me a small, tin sign from the 5 & 10—TEMPORARILY OUT OF ORDER. "I want them to see we have all the comforts of the big city."

The other furnishing in the outhouse was a well-stocked bookcase with all the latest copies of *Ballyhoo, Judge, The New Masses, The New Republic*, and a varied assortment of magazines of the early 1930s. My intellectual development at that time stopped at the *Ballyhoo* level, but I became very erudite from digesting accounts of the activities and sayings of one Elmer Zilch, *Ballyhoo's* symbolic boob. In the winter it was always a contest to see whether one's thirst for knowledge would outlast the fear of permanent genital frostbite. I should mention, out of fairness to my parents, that the inside facility was always available, but the price was a call to "man the pumps." Furthermore, the wisdom of Elmer Zilch was not available inside, having been banned on specific orders from Jean. For me, however, *Better Homes and Gardens* was hardly an acceptable substitute.

A more sociologically relevant experience in answering the call of nature was available at my Uncle Seymour's house up the road. Seymour lived in the old Barnes family homestead, which was built in the 1790s and added to from time to time, but never otherwise updated. The only facility was reached by going out the back door and into the garage, which had the granary on one side. Here the reading was limited to Sears Roebuck and "Monkey Ward" catalogues, which in the depth of the Depression in the farm belt, had an additional and rather unsatisfactory function. Once when I complained about the substitution to my uncle, I was directed to a pile of corncobs outside the garage. I mentioned my unhappiness at the alternatives to Dad somewhat later, but he responded with one of his typical monologues about 4 A.M. risings. I did note that he never visited Uncle Seymour's without packing a roll of paper in his hunting coat.

The other excitement related to Uncle Seymour's facility was its closeness to the granary and the constant gnawing of the rats, who would occasionally make an appearance through a hole in the floor. When one was seated, these noises produced a certain level of anxiety, which I understood far better years later when I was introduced to Professor Freud's concept of castration anxiety.

After one of the old rural schoolhouses nearby was demolished, an auction was held and, predictably, Dad was there. In addition to purchasing a desk, on which he claimed to have carved a girlfriend's initials during a lackluster sixth-grade class, he also bought the three-holer from the girls' outhouse. It was stored in the barn for a long time, and then suddenly I noted one morning that it, along with some fence posts, was gone. Soon Dad appeared with that look of pleased accomplishment on his face. "We won't have to waste any time shooting ducks anymore." And that was all he said as he rushed upstairs to start his morning writing—having already wasted some two hours with a phantom construction. He obviously didn't wish to be disturbed with questions at this point, so I started out on an exploration of my own, putting together the disappearance of the three-holer and the reference to duck shooting.

Directly behind our farm was the Owasco Outlet, referred to then as a stream, although in the West it would have been upgraded to the status of a major river. An abrupt drop-off from our land to the stream created a favorite hunting site for ducks; we could shoot at them as they made suicidal dashes up and down the outlet. My suspicion was correct—just within the tree line at the top of the drop, I found the three-holer sitting elegantly on four fence posts, with a fifth post strategically placed on the outlet side, to serve as a gun rest and to prevent a disastrous 100-foot drop on the part of the user into the stream below.

This bit of sanitation received very little use for the dual purpose for which it was designed. However, several years later Dad invited a group that he referred to as "big city intelligentsia"—New York literary and theatrical friends—for a weekend in the country. Before their arrival we were informed that the inside toilet and all the outside facilities were to be locked and that the guests were to be directed to the duck-hunting, three-holer as the only toilet on the farm. About all I remember of the episode was much loud, New York–style laughter, great consumption of a vast variety of drinks, and Dad enjoying the role of country bumpkin to its fullest. After the last bursts of laughter and subsided, the various facilities were ceremoniously unlocked. Luckily, in retrospect, no drunken literati were lost to the waters of the Owasco Outlet.

As a builder of rustic camps Dad had few equals, and each camp offered a welcome challenge to his abilities as a sanitarian. I asked him once where he had acquired these skills, and he indicated he had extensive training, including an engineering degree from the International Correspondence School of Scranton, Pennsylvania. When I later asked him (since he was an engineer) to help me learn how to use my slide rule, he was suddenly preoccupied elsewhere, and I never heard more of his engineering degree.

The line of Barnes forest cabins was started with the purchase of one on the edge of the Adirondack Mountains. It came equipped with an inside chemical toilet, which eliminated the need for Dad's sanitarian skills; he then demonstrated his unique interior decorating capabilities by appropriately embellishing the walls with colorful objects d'art. Directly facing the male user was a very large photograph of Alfred M. Landon, bidding for the viewer's vote for president. Still embedded in my cortex are the moving words inscribed below Alf's smiling face:

> That Leadership along the trail
> That we have loved long since,
> And lost a while,
> Has come to us again.

Unfortunately for the Republican Party, that leadership—loved though it was—led down the wrong trail and was lost again, with Mr. Landon carrying only Maine and Vermont in the 1936 fiasco. However, the trail of Barnes-built sanitary facilities plunged deeper and deeper into the upstate wilderness, only to be terminated decades later when Dad moved to the California coast. Stricter zoning there precluded the exercise of the engineering talents of this International Correspondence School graduate of 1906 vintage. By an act of fate, however, Hugh Hefner came along, and Dad appropriately exercised his interior decorating skills with Hef's centerfolds, which were displayed in the Barnes facilities. So, mercifully, the Great Sanitarian was allowed to complete a half-century's worth of contributions to the health and comfort of mankind from coast to coast.

Chapter 14
Dad Fights the
Great Depression

"Bo, you'll never taste a better sirloin than this," Dad announced as he came up from the cellar with a large glob of blackened meat securely pressed between the two sides of the hand-held, open-flame broiler. "It would cost you $5.50 at the Waldorf Astoria." My fantasies of dining in this quintessence of culinary luxury were constantly inflated by such references to the Waldorf and its famed chef, Oskar. For an eleven-year-old, whose dining exposure had been limited to Chang's Chinese Palace, reveries of such affluent ambience knew no bounds. However, the smell of burnt beef and the gas from burning coal that accompanied Dad's ascent from steak-broiling in the basement furnace erased any momentary dreams of spotless linens, hostesses in strapless silk evening gowns, and attentive waiters in tails. The effort of chewing charred steak from surplus Holstein milk cows further inhibited my fantasies of dining on "$5.50" steak at the Waldorf. Mom had the poor taste to complain about the charring, but Dad passed her grumbling off with some statement to the effect of "charcoal is good for the digestion." With this benediction, he left the tale with a final remark: "Grace, I'm having 4 tons of bootleg coal delivered tomorrow."

Although Dad had extinguished my Waldorf dreams for that night, he had suddenly planted the seeds of a new, more vivid one—bootleggers delivering coal! Bootleggers meant Al Capone, tommy guns, Packard touring cars, and St. Valentine's Day massacres in dingy garages. The next morning, a large, very dirty, broken-down Mack dump truck turned in the driveway and came to an abrupt stop with a loud squawk of the metal to metal from brake drums long since denuded by months of neglect. As I rushed to the window two very dirty, smallish men, with bib overalls and nondescript fabric coats slid down from broken remnants of what had once been a front seat. Bootleggers? No double-breasted black coats, gray leather gloves, and Knox homburgs to match their black shoes and gray spats? And worst of all, no tommy guns!

Dad was alerted to their arrival by the driver's attempt to slam the door on his side, which resulted in another prolonged but futile squawk, higher pitched and louder than the cry of pain from the tragically mutilated brake drums. Behind the safety of the living room window, I looked out as Dad greeted the men warmly, completed the agreement on price, showed them the appropriate cellar window for the delivery, and came back into the house. No altercation and no gunfire! "The poor bastards drove all night from Pennsylvania after digging that damn coal all afternoon from some abandoned mine, and all they get is $4 a ton. If they didn't bootleg it, the goddamned mine owners in Scranton would let them starve." That was my brief introduction to the Depression and economics.

The next thing I heard was Dad bellowing at Mom, "Grace, make a hell of a lot of strong coffee for these poor duffers, so when they're finished I can give them a jolt of coffee and a belly full of those 2-day-old crullers I got in Auburn yesterday." A half-hour later Dad ushered into the kitchen two of the dirtiest, most exhausted, and emaciated men I had ever seen, with coal-smeared faces and hands and carbon-impregnated clothes hanging from what must once have been well-muscled shoulders. They sopped their crullers in the large coffee mugs Dad filled again and again as they slowly relaxed. I don't remember much of the conversation, but it had to do with the sad fate of the mines and the upcoming election; Dad made some sarcastic remarks about where the hell were the chickens in every pot and what he irreverently referred to as "Hoover's Republican nonsense," a sentiment that seemed to get ready support from our now better-hydrated bootleggers. Apparently Dad was enjoying his audience sufficiently well that he broke out his ever-refillable bottle of high-proof kirschwasser, which was added to the coffee in generous portions. When the two bedraggled refugees from the Pennsylvania coalfields finally staggered out and fell into the devastation of what had once been a proud Mack truck, I had completed my first glimpses of the impact of the Great Depression. Dad's only comment as they left was "The poor bastards have a lot of guts trying to keep body and soul together. I wish I could have used 10 tons."

Dad always spoke of the Barnes family as being "biological Republicans." Upstate New York, until World War II, was staunchly Republican, and no Barnes, Short, or Storke was known to have Democratic leanings, and if they did, those inclinations must have been expressed in a traitorous manner in the secrecy of the voting booth. Dad's maternal grandfather, a major in Civil War General Phil Sheridan's cavalry, looked at Democrats as "rebels," "Cooperheads," and the like. Thus, when the most articulate member of the family came out as a vocal supporter of Roosevelt and the New Deal and even had the guts to publish a book titled *The Money Changers Versus The New Deal*[1], a silence fell over family gatherings; for some time, political issues were not discussed in Dad's presence. However, Uncle Jack Fitzgibbons, upstate's only Democratic congressman and my mother's relative, was not deterred from referring to FDR as a "demented victim of general paralysis of the insane." This diagnosis lost validity because it had only surfaced after the president "dumped" Uncle Jack for political disloyalty. Dad let the challenge from Mom's relative drop, being averse to face-to-face confrontations. I asked Dad why he hadn't defended the president, and he mumbled something about "your mother's family" and "Irish politicians" suffering from the "curse of the Irish"—whatever that was.

I realize now how fortunate we were during the Great Depression to be living on the upstate farm, far from the visual evidence of that financial and human debacle, so evident in the big cities like New York. Dad, who had a secure job and a good salary with Scripps-Howard newspapers in New York, split his time between the farm and New York City. One day he brought a delightful, unemployed young Italian couple to live with us for a number of months; they introduced me to Italian food, the love of which has never left me.

Not all Dad's many efforts to assist friends and relatives in coping with the ravages of the Depression resulted in such a positive culinary outcome. Dave Douglas, Dad's hunting companion, whose farm was across the Owasco Outlet from ours, had both a bumper crop of cabbage and a German wife who specialized in making sauerkraut. One day, Dave's old Chevy truck arrived with 20 bushels of cabbage and a large pile of straw. The cabbages were dumped by the side of the house and thoroughly covered with the straw, which was to serve as insulation against a winter freeze. The next day Dave's wife arrived with two of her teenage daughters, along with three large earthenware crocks, more cabbage, and other ingredients that I no longer remember. The final result was 50 gallons of sauerkraut. That evening Dad let it be known that "we'll have more goddamned corned beef and cabbage and wieners and sauerkraut than you can shake a stick at." The nausea produced by corned beef and cabbage had long since faded but the aversion lives on. And when the term "Kraut" was used to refer to Germans ten years later during World War II, it carried more than the usual negative connotation for me.

The Great Depression slowly dissolved as we moved into the late 1930s and then the relative prosperity of World War II. Dad's kind deeds to the less fortunate were never ending, but his editorial and oratorial support of the New Deal and FDR waned to the relief of his family on the farm, who were still blaming the president for "killing the little pigs."

Chapter 15
Great Barnes Projects
Dad as Straw Boss

"Jesus Christ, I said to get a good night's sleep, not to loll around in bed all day." And so, during a brief sojourn at home between my sophomore and junior year in college, we were awakened at 5:30 one June morning. One of my friends and I had helped Dad move a load of furniture from our old cabin in the Berkshires to a new one behind our Cooperstown houses. There was nothing remakable about the endeavor, except we had spent 48 endless hours loading and unloading old four-poster beds, ancient mattresses stained by generation of enuretic farm boys, piles of old copies of *Judge* and *Life* (the pre-Luce ones), and similar hoarded memorabilia. It was just another routine Barnes project. The two days had included 500 miles in the old Model A pickup that Dad had purchased after the phone company had squeezed it for 400,000 miles on the back roads of upstate New York. He had painted it bright crimson and pronounced it "the best goddamned Ford old Henry ever made." During these 48 hours we had been nourished with 4 bottles of Ballantyne ale, 8 cups of black, instant coffee, and 4 large, dry peanut butter sandwiches constructed with stale rye bread. What had sustained us was the encouraging word, "You'll all have one helluva long sleep when you get home." His effervescent awakening call at 5:30 the next morning capped that long sleep at a restful 4 hours! Such is my memory of a typical Great Barnes Project.

The old saw "You can take the farm boy out of the farm but you can't take the farm out of the boy" was played out to its fullest in Dad. He was constantly planning building projects, usually for someone else to build, not because he eschewed hard physical labor but because of his myriad other activities. When he did add to the effort, or promised to, we quietly groaned. He referred to himself as a "crapdoodle carpenter," which was indeed a more than charitable appellation for his avocation. The frugality of the American farmer on the frontier usually came to the fore—never buy new lumber if you can find some bankrupt soul demolishing his barn or cowshed. Nothing was more characteristic of these purchases than floorboards stained with a half-century of the excrement of generations of Herefords. When he then matched and sawed these with the care and alacrity of Genghis Khan breaching the gates of Christendom, the product was indeed unique. And so, when we heard a loud "Boys, here's what we're going to do!" followed by "YOU do your best to finish it up by Friday," we were greatly relieved, even though "by Friday" imposed a schedule as unrealistic as the magnitude of the project. At least, the "YOU" predicted the effort would preclude his involvement, thus ensuring some protection of our very limited sense of esthetics and our life and limb from the potential of structural collapse.

Occasionally we were buttressed in these efforts by an unemployed, alcoholic, 75-year-old carpenter known affectionately as Jeppo. "Keep the old boy stoked up with hard cider and we'll get a hell of a lot of work out of him." (In 1935 the concepts of alcohol rehabilitation and the evils of booze and drugs in the workplace were not front-burner issues, particularly on Barnes construction endeavors.) The projects themselves were as varied as Dad's moods and imagination. They ranged from rugged hunting lodges to small "view platforms" overlooking lake vistas, mountain panoramas, and secret game trails. Dad imagined that in deer season, the trails would be packed with thousands of deer, "like the goddamn migrating caribou in Alaska." No deer were ever seen from any of these platforms; nor were any nimrods ever recruited to man these facilities.

The lodge constructions usually carried a time

schedule of two weeks. Supplies included an admixture of "fine antique" remnants of siding, beams, and
uriniferous floorboards buttressed by a sparse supply
of new lumber to be used only when necessary for
health and sanitation purposes. These purposes were
clearly defined to exclude anything other than outhouse seats. Major lodge projects called for the special
skills of Jeppo, and the time line precluded Dad's active involvement. However, in these situations he was
indeed the Straw Boss incarnate, with his engineer
boots and stern advice to all involved in such critical
activities. Two or three visits during the two-week
construction period were usually adequate to con-
vince the Straw Boss that all was progressing according to his schedule and "on budget" and that Jeppo
was well-enough lubricated to ensure that his 75-
year-old body still exuded some of the enthusiasm
salvaged from his misspent youth. In the words of the
old Straw Boss, "Jeppo's had more women and booze
in his 75 years than Al Capone and Warren G.
Harding rolled into one." And thus we were incul-
cated with ideas of women and drinking vastly out of
tune with the feminism and the co-dependency evils
of alcoholism of the 1990s.

Because we usually found ourselves several days
behind on our two-week's construction deadline
when the Straw Boss made his final inspection, we
were faced with a frenetic two-day "catch up," which
involved eighteen-hour days and required light to be
provided by soot-laden kerosene lanterns. We were

cheered on by the enthusiastic voice of the Straw Boss, now part of the construction team. "Boys, we'll meet the goddamn schedule yet, and then we'll have a hell of a big sirloin and wash it down with some whiskey that will bring tears to Jeppo's eyes and a fire to his guts!" By this time Jeppo was dragging his small 5-foot, 3-inch frame, along with a couple of long 4 x 4's with an alacrity that today would have had any sensible mortician activating the beeper of his favorite embalmer. Somewhere inside, the old boy discovered a last remnant of energy and outlasted all of us, including the Straw Boss.

The last few hours of any lodge-building project consisted of finding some decorative or utilitarian purpose for any pieces of unused lumber. "There's no damn reason to cart all this good lumber home." And so the lodge was usually surrounded by picnic tables (often of very uncertain shape and unequal stance), shooting platforms on nearby trees (just in case "the damn deer overrun the place"), and an extra three-holer without roof or sides and with seat constructed from the rough side of ancient siding ("just in case some old codger has a prune juice alert"). Actually I think that Dad had a vision of himself sitting comfortably on one of these outside thrones and shooting a stray buck. He seldom ventured to one of these facilities without having a .30-06 readily at hand.

The final touch came on the last day, usually after midnight, and always within the original time frame set by the Straw Boss. ("Neither rain, nor snow, nor

Another cabin in the wilderness

ice" deferred the wrap-up on the appointed date.) Jeppo would be making a valiant attempt to hang the front door in the frame the Straw Boss, momentarily turned carpenter, had just finished: "Don't worry, Jeppo, if it's just a little bit off. It'll last until Hell freezes over." We would be directed toward crucial last-minute tasks—sweeping the accumulation of decades of cow dung from the floor of what would euphemistically be called the front porch and picking up odd remnants of lumber left over from the frenetic, last-minute construction of outlying tables, benches, and three-holers. And then suddenly the sky would be lighted by a fireball concocted from aged lumber ends, sawdust, and kerosene—all ignited by the Straw Boss, about to be transformed from Carpenter to Master Chef and Bartender.

The Master Chef had salvaged a shelf from an old ice box on one of his trips to a junkyard, during which he excavated items to add to the luxury of the various cabins and lodges even though these structures were but visions in his fertile imagination. The shelves would be placed between rocks scrounged for the occasion. Combustible material, gathered from the remnants of the week's activities, burned fiercely with the addition of kerosene and gave forth an aroma that seemed reminiscent of the Chicago fire of 1871, started after Mrs. O'Reilly's cow kicked over the lantern. The linkage was not lost on the Master Chef who would be quick to announce, "Savor this sirloin, boys. It's got the flavor of the Chicago stockyards." And, indeed, we would have ambivalently noted the odor exuding from the fire had not the Chef previously performed in his other role to close out this two weeks' adventure—Bartender. The contents of large bottle of Calvert Reserve had been poured into an odd collection of jelly glasses, which were passed to us even before the sirloin was placed over the full-flavored flame. By the time the quart of Calvert had disappeared, we were more than ready to accept the Chef's compliments to himself, "Boys, you couldn't get a tasty steak like this in the Pump Room or the Drake." And so another Barnes project was completed, and we awaited the Straw Boss's metamorphosis into the Great Interior Decorator.

Chapter 16
The Last Toast

As it must to all men, time ran out on Dad as he was about to enter his eightieth year. Whether it was unusually robust genes or his pious mother's intervention with one of the Holy Trinity, he had been granted ten years beyond the biblically alloted three score and ten. As he would have put it himself, he was "snatched by the Lord" on a beautiful August morning in 1968 as he arose from the breakfast table. He was characteristically absorbed in entertaining his guests at that last breakfast and boomed out a toast carrying a message deemed worthy of more than parochial interest: "To Richard Milhous Nixon, may the son . . ." These were certified by Jean to have been his last words. They were emphatically punctuated with a finality underlined by the shattering of his wine glass and a brief cascade of his favorite chablis, fresh from the vineyard of Ernest and Julio, flowing off the table and onto the bare floor under his chair. He slumped slowly downward, coming peacefully to rest near the front legs of the antique table that served as a sideboard. It supported an assortment of pictures, including those of the 1926 Rolls, the Big Hupp, Jean with the midget pointers Dianne and Voltman, My Sin and Mr. Cat, and a faded photograph of a Barnes family reunion at the Old Homestead, circa 1899.

Why would toasting Richard Milhous Nixon on the occasion of his nomination as Republican candidate for president arouse, within Dad's sympathetic nervous system, a storm severe enough to disrupt the orderly contraction and relaxation of his myocardium? The situation seems, on the surface, paradoxical: Dad had often proclaimed himself a "biological Republican" from upstate New York, who had developed a deep visceral dislike for the new breed of liberal Democrats and what he saw as their addiction to "perpetual war for perpetual peace."[1] Certainly his vast knowledge of politics and its practitioners left him with few illusions as to their honesty and devotion to the national interest, over and above personal glorification. Why then such feelings toward a supposedly conservative Republican and a well-known career politician?

In truth, his reaction came from the heart of an idealistic student infused with the deeply rooted faith of a nineteenth-century farm boy in the American way of life. Engrafted on this base, by his years of education and experience, was an optimistic hope that a rational and humane application of science could and would bring to America a utopian century. He ranted and raved against the cupidity and stupidity of the world as he saw it; yet he never lost faith in some ultimate salvation of mankind. That driving force came from the wellspring of his early pioneer, rural, fundamentalist upbringing and the simple faith of his devout mother. In his mind he knew this belief was all fantasy, but in his heart of hearts he kept the faith. Those who would pervert or destroy it were his enemies. And high on this list in 1968 was Richard Nixon.

Dad was, in truth, the "learned crusader," as named in the title of his biography.[2] "Yes, Mother Barnes, your favorite son did not forsake Christ but with his last breath sought to exorcise a money changer from the Temple." And so HEB departed, leaving a legacy of memories of America during the nineteenth and early twentieth century—memories that live on in me and my children and the many fortunate individuals who were touched by his vitality, heady humor, and personal warmth.

Chapter 17
H.E.B.—
His Family Legacy
Thoughts for
His Grandchildren

The day he died, his grandchildren had yet to be born. Mark was zero minus 50-some days old and Robin had not even been considered. As I sat quietly sobbing on that half-filled 707, heading back to San Antonio after his funeral, I was enveloped with the empty feeling that I had heard for the last time his cheerful, "Bo, come on out. This will just take a minute." No more summons to one of those ten-hour marathon clean-up jobs stacking wood, weeding gardens, or picking up fallen apples for the cider mill. And no more loud explosions from the kitchen: "Jean, where did you put the goddamn Hupmobile keys?" or "Bo, get the hell down here and clean up the kitchen, and we'll go to town for a chocolate ice cream cone." (In Dad's mind there was only one ice cream flavor, chocolate, and to risk ordering something else was an admission of imbecilic judgment, an act never ventured.)

The flight attendant's warning to fasten seat belts "for our descent into San Antonio" broke up my tearful reminiscing, the first real chance I had given myself to feel the sadness and emptiness that would be with me from time to time in the years ahead. A sensitive and feeling man, Dad had always kept his own losses and griefs shielded from public and even family view and had willed the donning of that same demeanor to me, his only son. Even when his beloved mother died, he seemed to pass off his grief with the off-hand remark, "Now she can read her Bible in the lap of Jesus."

Yes, Mark and Robin, had he lived another decade you wold have clear memories of him. Then you would have been eight and ten. How would you have seen him? Bent and aged, given to long stories after dinner about people and events ages past and the expression of strong views about almost everything? No, he wouldn't have jounced either of you on his knee, nor would he have been likely to bring you presents when he came to visit. He might have appeared to ignore you soon after you came to visit him at Malibu. But he would have proudly shown your pictures to all who came to the Rancho to visit and would have sung warmly of your good looks and quiet demeanor. "They're a hell of a lot better behaved than most kids today." When he felt comfortable with you, he would have grabbed a gun and a walking stick and taken you around the gardens and up to the top of the hill and pointed out Catalina Island emerging in the distance from the afternoon's Pacific mist. Then he would have pointed out the old lumber pile where he had executed "two of the biggest goddamned rattlesnakes ever seen in this part of the country."

On the way back he would have taken you into his office, exuding the musty aroma of old books and papers, all laden with layers of dust. He would have shown you some of the hundreds of pictures tacked to the walls, particularly pictures of his father, H. L. Mencken, the Stone House in Cooperstown, and himself at the wheel of the Rolls Royce. (You also might have spied numerous photographs of thinly clad women about whom you would not have dared inquire.) Yes, you would have remembered this quaint old man, by then in his late eighties, and thought him very unlike anyone you had ever met before. You would have had difficulty connecting those impressions with stories I have told you of him as you have grown older.

An optimistic stance was characteristic of much of Dad's approach to life, tempered with a strong touch of cynicism as he became older and suffered more disappointments. He had a deep-seated faith in scientific advances and man's ability to apply them to solve our morass of social and economic difficulties. This inordinate belief in scientific "experts" was mixed with a skepticism that the "voice of the common man" had much to contribute. His strong aversion to the jury system was an example of this thinking. He also had a deep mistrust of elected officials. Yet, on a different tack, he saw himself as one of the common folk, being proud of his relatively humble, rural origins and not in the least given to putting on airs. He would listen attentively and courteously to any grocery clerk or gas station attendant who had an opinion to express. Later, he might quietly remark to me, "He's got some jackass ideas."

Although he rejected conventional, organized religion and publicly debated its tenets with notable clerics, he held closely to the Judeo-Christian ethic of hard work, honesty, and most of the directives of at least nine of the Ten Commandments. He was very much his own man and would often stand on principle, particularly on political and academic issues, much to the detriment of his own professional and financial advancement. His thinking was often on the cutting edge in areas of social and economic policy; yet much of his personal life-style was more characteristic of a nineteenth-century rural American than of twentieth-century futurist.

He hewed to no clear ideological path politically. He was one of the founders of the New School for Social Research, a very liberal, avant-garde educational experiment when first established. He worked closely with Roger Baldwin after the founding of the American Civil Liberties Union and was a close friend and companion on the speaking circuit of Clarence Darrow. His column in Scripps-Howard was called *The Liberal Viewpoint*. He frequently shared the podium congenially with Norman Thomas, perennial candidate for president on the Socialist ticket. Yet in later life, he was admired by many conservative groups and was highly skeptical of Keynesian economic policies that he saw leading to increasing deficits.

He was a handsome man who possessed considerable charisma. Yet he never seemed aware of his good looks, nor used his appearance to impress or manipulate others, with the probable exception of selected members of the coterie of women he often attracted. He was courteous to a fault in face-to-face contacts. Yet if his feathers were ruffled by some poor soul's off-hand remark, the old Underwood would burst forth with a fusillade of devastating magnitude. However, he never held a grudge. That same individual might have been invited the following week to drop in for cocktails and would then have been greeted as an esteemed brother. Always being careful to separate the man from his thinking, he would likely remark subsequently, "He's a cultured gent but he's got the wisdom of a Neanderthal boob."

He was often generous to a fault, although the gifts so generously bestowed were varied and at times not wholly welcome. Guests, including unmarried couples, were often jovially greeted at sunrise by the Inspector General (Jean's term for him on such occasions), who invaded their bedroom with vast flagons of hot coffee. The beverage was invariably brewed with sufficient powdered Antigua to either stimulate the colon into immediate action or flush the kidneys with a cascade reminiscent of Niagara Falls. The coffee was accompanied by large, two-day-old bear claws or mammoth crullers. Sometimes the lady was awarded a cymbidium from one of his Malibu gardens.

He was legend in Cooperstown for delivering 12-foot blue spruces to innumerable friends at Christmas time; the trees were products of thinning operations at his Stonewood nursery. Cymbidium orchids and Birds of Paradise were lavished on Malibu friends after Dad and Jean moved to the coast. His habit of dispensing generous drinks at cocktail hour was a source of wonder and often despair, particularly when he was going through a phase of featuring Zombies, a large mixture of rum, anisette, fruit juices, and other unknown intoxicants.

Although Dad amassed a significant financial estate from his massive efforts through the years, he was never in any sense wealthy. Major purchases were made through the Sears catalogue and discount and factory outlet stores. He experienced many financial losses in publishing ventures and stock investments throughout the 1930s and 1940s. Although he never admitted it publicly and often blamed others, it must have been clear to him that as informed as he was in academic economics, he lacked an elemental business sense. Whether he was betrayed by his trusting nature, his overgrown optimism, or a congenital lack of interest in business details is unclear. With all his losses and relative dearth of financial rewards for his incredible productivity (much of it first class), his bitterness was well tempered by his sense of humor and deep enjoyment of his life and work. As in Frank Sinatra's song of the 1950s "I Did It My Way," his rewards were in the doing of it—always his way.

It has been difficult, Mark and Robin, even now when you are both into your twenties, to interest you in your Grandfather Barnes and the extent of his monumental endeavors. It would be impossible to indicate to you the effect on your own father of having a dad who was one of the significant intellectual and public figures of his youth. Mark, you may have experienced a touch of this influence when your elderly history professor asked why you—an undergraduate economics major—were taking history courses. Being at a loss, you mentioned that your grandfather was a historian. When learning your grandfather's name, his face took on a faraway look and he uttered an impressed "When I was a student, he was The Authority!"

In the words of the characters in an old-time radio soap opera, *Vic and Sade,* "You take the bitter with the better." Or to quote another cliche from "The Golden Age of Radio," "You play with the hand you're dealt." And for me the hand was pretty good, and the "better" far outweighed the "bitter." Like many children of celebrities—in this case an only son—beliefs, attitudes, and subsequent life choices contain an admixture of emulation and revolt. And so it was with me. And, Mark and Robin, so it has been and will continue to be with you. This is the way a current generation of parents, and those generations that came before, affect the new arrivals. This is how your grandfather has already, and will in the years ahead, profoundly affect your lives, even though you never met.

You, as his grandchildren, may see many of these conflicting characteristics, the admixture of emulation and revolt, in your own father, his son. And your children may someday try to fathom similar inconsistencies in you. Yet, those around you will be well served should your grandfather's influence have endowed you with an abundant strain of his generosity, honesty, humor, and modesty, not to mention his energy and creativity.

Notes

Introduction

1. Clarence Day, *Life with Father* (New York: Alfred A. Knopf, 1935).

2. Fredrick Lewis Allen, *Only Yesterday* (New York: Harper & Row, 1959).

3. Fredrick Lewis Allen, *Since Yesterday* (New York: Harper & Row, 1968).

4. Harry Elmer Barnes, *The Genesis of the World War* (New York: Alfred A. Knopf, 1926).

5. Harry Elmer Barnes, *The Twilight of Christianity* (New York: Vanguard Press, 1929).

Chapter 4

1. Harry Elmer Barnes, *Prohibition versus Civilization* (New York, Viking Press, 1932).

Chapter 10

I am indebted to Ray C. Turnbaugh, Ph.D., for several of the following references, which he located in the Barnes Collection housed in the American Heritage Center, University of Wyoming, Laramie. These were included in his unpublished doctoral thesis, "Harry Elmer Barnes: The Quest for Truth and Justice," University of Illinois, Urbana-Champaign, 1977.

1. Harry Elmer Barnes, Letter to Gov. Edmund Brown, June 1, 1959, Barnes Collection.

2. Ibid., October 23, 1959.

3. Harry Elmer Barnes to Max Lerner, October 23, 1959, Barnes Papers.

4. Harry Elmer Barnes, *History and Social Intelligence* (New York: Alfred A. Knopf, 1926), p. 456.

5. Harry Elmer Barnes, "The Liberal Viewpoint," *New York World-Telegram*, July 23, 1932, Barnes Papers.

6. Harry Elmer Barnes, *Los Angeles Examiner*, July 10, 1923, Barnes Papers.

7. Ibid.

8. Harry Elmer Barnes, "Education vs. Enlightenment" in *The New Generation*, V. F. Calverton, ed. (New York, Macauly Co., 1930), p. 644.

9. Ibid., p. 651.

10. Harry Elmer Barnes, *The Twilight Versus Civilization* (New York: Viking Press, 1932), p. 41.

11. Ibid.

12. Harry Elmer Barnes, *Prohibition Versus Civilization* (New York: Viking Press, 1932), p. 41.

13. Ibid., p. 21.

Chapter 14

1. Harry Elmer Barnes, *The Money Changers Versus The New Deal* (New York: Long and Smith, 1934).

Chapter 16

1. Harry Elmer Barnes ed., *Perpetual War for Perpetual Peace* (Caldwell, Id.: Caxton Publisher, Ltd., 1953).

2. Arthur Goddard ed., *Learned Crusader* (Colorado Springs, Colo.: Ralph Myles, Publisher, Inc., 1968).